The *Oxford Progressive English Readers* series provides a wide range of reading for learners of English.

Each book in the series has been written to follow the strict guidelines of a syllabus, wordlist and structure list. The texts are graded according to these guidelines; Grade 1 at a 1,400 word level, Grade 2 at a 2,100 word level, Grade 3 at a 3,100 word level, Grade 4 at a 3,700 word level and Grade 5 at a 5,000 word level.

The latest methods of text analysis, using specially designed software, ensure that readability is carefully controlled at every level. Any new words which are vital to the mood and style of the story are explained within the text, and reoccur throughout for maximum reinforcement. New language items are also clarified by attractive illustrations.

Each book has a short section containing carefully graded exercises and controlled activities, which test both global and specific understanding.

The Stalled Ox and Other Stories

Saki

1993
Hong Kong
Oxford University Press
Oxford Singapore Tokyo

Oxford University Press

Oxford New York Toronto
Kuala Lumpur Singapore Hong Kong Tokyo
Delhi Bombay Calcutta Madras Karachi
Nairobi Dar es Salaam Cape Town
Melbourne Auckland Madrid

and associated companies in
Berlin Ibadan

Oxford is a trade mark of Oxford University Press

First published 1993

© Oxford University Press 1993

All rights reserved. No part of this publication may be reproduced, stored in a retrieval system, or transmitted, in any form or by any means, without the prior permission in writing of Oxford University Press (Hong Kong) Ltd. Within Hong Kong, exceptions are allowed in respect of any fair dealing for the purpose of research or private study, or criticism or review, as permitted under the Copyright Ordinance currently in force. Enquiries concerning reproduction outside these terms and in other countries should be sent to Oxford University Press (Hong Kong) Ltd at the address below

This book is sold subject to the condition that it shall not, by way of trade or otherwise, be lent, re-sold, hired out or otherwise circulated without the publisher's prior consent in any form of binding or cover other than that in which it is published and without a similar condition including this condition being imposed on the subsequent purchaser

Illustrated by K.Y. Chan

Syllabus designer: David Foulds

Text processing and analysis by Luxfield Consultants Ltd.

ISBN 0 19 585383 0

Printed in Hong Kong
Published by Oxford University Press (Hong Kong) Ltd
18/F Warwick House, Tong Chong Street, Quarry Bay, Hong Kong

CONTENTS

1	AWKWARD HABITS	1
2	CLOVIS SANGRAIL AND FRIENDS	12
3	THE HOUNDS OF FATE	26
4	WILD BOYS	35
5	ANXIOUS MOMENTS	48
6	THE REMOULDING OF GROBY LINGTON	58
7	TROUBLESOME TIMES	68
8	A QUIET LIFE	79
9	THE WAY TO THE DAIRY	91
10	LIFE'S LITTLE PROBLEMS	99
11	THE SPECIALISTS	109
	QUESTIONS AND ACTIVITIES	117

1

AWKWARD HABITS

THE STALLED OX

The painter

Theophil Eshley was an artist by profession. He was very good at his work, and could paint any subject he could think of, but circumstances had forced him to specialize in pictures of cows.

On one side of his garden there was a small field in which a neighbour kept some small cows. At noon in summer-time the cows stood deep in tall grass under the shade of a group of trees, with spots of sunlight falling on their smooth brown backs. Eshley had once painted a beautiful picture of two peaceful-looking cows under a green tree with the grass and sunlight all round them. The Royal Academy had chosen it for its Summer Exhibition.

The Royal Academy, the most respected authority of its kind in the country, likes its artists to be orderly. If they are good at painting one sort of picture, then that is the kind of picture they should stick to. Eshley had painted a successful picture of two brown cows sleeping prettily under a green tree, and as he had begun, so he went on. His 'Peace at Noon-time,' showing two brown cows under a green tree, was followed by 'A Midday Rest,' a painting of a green tree, with two brown cows under it. After that there came 'Cool Shadows,' 'Quiet Cow' and 'A Dream in Dairyland,' all of which were pictures of green trees and brown cows.

His two attempts to paint something different were terrible failures: 'Birds Frightened by Eagle' and 'Wolves in the Italian Countryside' were not approved by the Academy and returned. Eshley then produced 'A Shaded Corner Where Sleepy Cows Stand Dreaming,' and was back in favour once more.

Adela Pingsford's problem

On a fine afternoon in late autumn, he was finishing off a picture of grass when his neighbour, Adela Pingsford, began knocking very loudly on his door.

'There is an ox in my garden,' she announced, explaining her noisy entrance.

'An ox,' said Eshley rather foolishly. He could not imagine why Adela should want to tell him such a thing. 'What kind of ox?'

'Oh, I don't know what kind,' answered the lady angrily. 'Just an ordinary ox. What I don't like about it is that it is in my garden. I have spent two weeks in that garden, getting it neat and tidy for the winter. An ox walking about in it won't help things. Besides, it is treading on the flowers.'

'How did it get into the garden?' asked Eshley.

'I think it came in by the gate,' said the lady impatiently. 'It couldn't have climbed over the walls and I don't think anyone dropped it from an aeroplane. The important question is not how it got in, but how to get it out.'

'Won't it go by itself?' said Eshley.

'If it wanted to go by itself,' said Adela Pingsford rather angrily, 'I should not have come here to talk to you about it. I'm nearly all alone; the servant is having her afternoon off and the cook is in bed with a headache. At school they may have taught us how to remove a large ox from a small garden, I suppose, but if they did, I cannot remember what they said. All I could think of was that you were a near neighbour and a person who paints cows. I thought that you must be familiar with the subjects that you painted, and that you might be of some help. Possibly I was wrong.'

'I paint dairy cows, certainly,' admitted Eshley, 'but I do not have any experience in dealing with wandering oxen. I've seen how cowboys do it in movies of course, but they always have horses and lots of other equipment.'

Adela Pingsford said nothing. She led the way to her garden. It normally seemed a fair-sized garden, but it looked very small with the ox standing in it. The ox was a huge animal. It was dull red about the head and shoulders, dirty white on the back legs, and it had large red eyes. It was as similar to the pretty milk cows that Eshley painted as the chief of a wild tribe of savages is to a Japanese tea-shop girl. Eshley stood very near the gate while he studied the animal's appearance and behaviour. Adela Pingsford continued to say nothing.

'It's eating a flower,' said Eshley at last.

'How clever you are,' said Adela. 'You seem to notice everything. As a matter of fact, it has got six flowers in its mouth at the present moment.'

The ox moves

Something had to be done. Eshley took a step or two in the direction of the animal, clapped his hands, and made noises like 'Hish' and 'Shoo'. If the ox heard them, it seemed to take no notice.

'If any hens should ever wander into my garden,' said Adela, 'I shall certainly come and ask you to frighten them out. You "shoo" beautifully. Meanwhile, do you mind trying to drive that ox away? That is my best rose bush that he's begun to eat now,' she added in a calm but icy voice, as a beautiful orange-coloured rose was crushed into the huge mouth.

Then Adela Pingsford's patience and icy calmness broke down. The language she used sent the artist a few feet nearer to the ox. He picked up a thin stick and flung it against the animal's legs. For a long moment, the ox stopped turning roses into lunch while it looked with great interest at the stick-thrower. Adela glared with equal interest and more obvious anger at the same person.

As the animal neither lowered its head nor stamped its feet, Eshley tried throwing another stick. The ox seemed to realize at once that it was being asked to move. It gave a hurried final bite at the flowers, and walked quickly up the garden. Eshley ran to turn it back towards the gate, but only succeeded in making it walk faster in the opposite direction.

oon, it had crossed a small area of grass between garden and house and pushed its way through the open French windows into the morning-room. Some flowers stood in vases around the room, and the animal continued its lunch. Meanwhile, Eshley imagined that a slightly dangerous look had come into its eyes. He stopped trying to make it go where it did not want to go.

Eshley gets his equipment

'Mr Eshley,' said Adela in a shaking voice, 'I asked you to drive that ox out of my garden, but I did not ask you to drive it into my house. If I must have it somewhere on my property, I prefer it to be in the garden than in the morning-room.'

'Cattle-driving is not my profession,' said Eshley. 'If I remember rightly, I told you so at the beginning.'

'I quite agree,' answered the lady. 'Painting pretty pictures of pretty little cows is what you're good at. Perhaps you'd like to do a nice one of that ox having lunch in my morning-room?'

Eshley immediately began walking away.

'Where are you going?' screamed Adela.

'To fetch my equipment,' was the answer.

'Equipment? I don't want you to start using a rope. Everything in the room will be destroyed if there's a struggle.'

But the artist marched out of the garden. In a couple of minutes he returned, with a stool, and his painting things.

'Do you mean to say that you're going to sit down quietly and paint that animal while it's destroying my morning-room?' gasped Adela.

'It was your idea,' said Eshley, setting his things in place.

'I won't allow it — I absolutely won't allow it!' screamed Adela.

'I don't see that there is anything you can do about it,' said the artist. 'It's not even your ox. Also, you seem to forget that the cook has a headache. She may be just falling asleep and your screaming will wake her up. You should think more of other people.'

'The man is mad!' exclaimed Adela. A moment later it was Adela herself who appeared to go mad. The ox had finished the flowers and the cover of a book. It appeared to be thinking of leaving the rather small room. Eshley noticed its restlessness and threw in some more flowers from the garden to keep it inside the room.

'I shall go to the Public Library and get them to telephone for the police,' said Adela, and she left.

Success

Some minutes later, the ox stepped carefully out of the morning-room, stared seriously at the human, who no longer bothered it with sticks, and then walked heavily but quickly through the garden gate. Eshley packed up his equipment and followed.

It was the turning-point in Eshley's artistic life. His amazing picture, 'Ox in a Morning-room, Late Autumn,' was one of the most talked-about works of the next Paris Art Exhibition, and when it was exhibited at Munich, it was bought by the German Government.

From that moment he was known everywhere as a successful painter. He could paint any subject he liked. Two years later, even the Royal Academy was happy to give a great space on its walls to his large painting, 'African Apes Wrecking a Bedroom.'

Eshley presented Adela Pingsford with a new copy of the book the ox had eaten and a couple of fine flowering plants for her garden, but she has never forgiven him.

A Holiday Task

Lunch at the Golden Galleon

Kenelm Jerton entered the dining room of the Golden Galleon Hotel at the busiest part of the lunch hour. The place was full of guests and visitors. Small extra tables had been brought in, so that many of the tables were almost touching each other.

Jerton was shown by a waiter to the only table that remained empty. He sat down with the uncomfortable and ridiculous feeling that everyone in the room was staring at him. He was a young man of ordinary appearance and quiet behaviour, but he felt that people always looked at him as though he were a famous man or a crazy one. After he had ordered his lunch, he stared at the flowers on his table and was stared at (or so he imagined) by several young ladies, some older women and an evil-looking businessman. He tried to ignore these thoughts, and began to take a special interest in the flowers.

'What is the name of those roses, do you know?' he asked the waiter. If the waiter wasn't able to answer a question about the food or the wine, he would never say so. But he was not ashamed to tell Jerton, and everyone else around, that he knew nothing about the names of roses.

'Amy Silvester Partington,' said a voice at Jerton's side.

The voice came from a pleasant faced, well-dressed young woman who was sitting at a table that almost touched Jerton's. He thanked her rather hurriedly and shyly for the information, and made some remark about the unusual colour of the flowers.

'It is a strange thing,' said the young woman, 'that I should be able to tell you the name of those roses without any difficulty. But if you ask me my own name, I shall be completely unable to give it to you.'

Jerton had not even thought of asking the woman her name. After her rather amazing announcement, however, he felt he had to say something to be polite.

Lady Somebody-or-other

'Yes,' answered the young woman, 'I suppose it is loss of memory — not complete, you know, but only partial. This morning I suddenly found myself in a train coming down here; my ticket told me that I had come from Victoria Station and was going to this place. I had a little money on me, but no name cards or any other clue to my identity, and no idea about who I was. Now the only thing I can remember about myself is that I have a title. I am Lady Somebody-or-other. Beyond that my mind is a blank.'

'What about luggage?' suggested Jerton, trying to be helpful. 'If you looked through your suitcases, you might find something that would tell you who you are.'

'I didn't have any with me,' the woman explained. 'I knew the name of this hotel and made up my mind to come here. When the hotel porter who meets the trains asked if I had any luggage, I made up a story about a small case — it's so embarrassing, you know, coming to a hotel without luggage. I pretended I had lost it. I told him my name was Smith. Soon he returned from a large pile of luggage carrying a small case labelled "Kestrel-Smith". I had to take it; I don't see what else I could have done.'

Jerton said nothing. But he wondered what the real owner of the case would think.

'Of course it was terrible arriving at a strange hotel with the name of Kestrel-Smith. But it would have been worse to have arrived without any luggage at all. Anyhow, I hate causing trouble.'

Jerton thought of all the hotel and railway officials who would by now be trying to help the Kestrel-Smiths find their lost case, but he said nothing. The lady continued to tell her story.

'Naturally, none of my keys would fit the locks, but I told the hotel porter that I had lost my key ring, and he had the locks broken open. The Kestrel-Smith's soap and things aren't the sort that I would ever buy, myself, but they are better than nothing.'

The negative method

Jerton had heard enough about the Kestrel-Smiths. He tried to change the subject.

'If you feel sure that you have a title,' he said, 'your name must be in Debrett's List. The name of everyone with a title is in that. Why don't you go to the library and see if they have a copy?'

'I did. But a mere book of names tells you awfully little, you know. If you were an army officer and had lost your identity, you might stare at the Army List for months without finding out who you were. I'm using a different method; I'm trying to find out by various little tests who I am not. You may have noticed, for instance, that I'm eating lobster.'

Jerton had not noticed this at all.

'It's one of the most expensive dishes on the menu and I can't really afford it, but it proves that I'm not Lady Starping;

she never eats seafood. And poor Lady Braddleshrub has a very bad stomach. If I am her, I shall certainly die in great pain some time this afternoon, and the duty of finding out who I am will fall on the newspapers and the police and those sort of people. By then I shall not care who I am. Lady Knewford doesn't know one rose from another and she hates men; she wouldn't have been able to tell you the name of that rose, and anyway she wouldn't have spoken to you. And Lady Mousehilton talks to every man she meets — you wouldn't say I was that sort of woman, would you?'

Jerton quickly told her she was not.

'Well, you see,' continued the lady, 'that knocks four off the list at once.'

'It'll take a long time to bring the list down to one,' said Jerton.

'Oh, but of course, there are lots of them that I couldn't possibly be — women who've got grandchildren or older children. I've only got to consider the women of about my own age. I tell you how you might help me this afternoon, if you don't mind. Go into the hotel smoking-room and look through the copies of *Country Life* and any other magazines they have there. Most magazines usually have at least a few photographs of Lady This or Lady That at some party or opening ceremony or something. See if you can find a picture of me. It will only take you ten minutes. I'll meet you in the lounge about tea-time. Thanks very much.'

And Lady Unknown, having forced Jerton into the search for her lost identity, rose and left the room. As she passed the young man's table, she stopped for a moment and whispered,

'Did you notice that I gave the waiter a one shilling tip? We can cross Lady Ulwight off the list; she would have died rather than give that much.'

The plan

At five o'clock Jerton went to the hotel lounge; he had spent an unsuccessful fifteen minutes among the magazines in the smoking-room. His new friend was seated at a small tea-table, with a waiter standing nearby.

'Have you discovered anything?' he asked.

'Only that I'm not Lady Befnal. She disapproves of any form of gambling, but I just put ten pounds on a horse called 'The Unknown' in the three-fifteen race. I suppose it was the name that attracted me.'

'Did it win?' asked Jerton.

'No, it came in second, the most annoying thing a horse can do when you've bet on it to come in first. Anyhow, I know now that I'm not Lady Befnal.'

'It seems to me that it cost a lot to learn that,' said Jerton.

'Well, yes, I've hardly anything left,' admitted the identity-seeker. 'The lobster made my lunch an expensive one, too. I've got rather a useful idea, though. I feel certain that I belong to the Pivot Club. I'll go back to London and ask the Club porter if there are any letters for me. He knows all the members by sight, and if there are any letters or telephone messages waiting for me, of course that will solve the problem. If he says there aren't any, I shall say, "You do know who I am, don't you?" and make him say what he thinks my name is. So I'll find out even if there is nothing for me to collect.'

The plan seemed a good one.

'Of course,' said the lady, 'I shall need my train fare back to London, and some money for my bill here and cabs and things. If you lend me three pounds, that ought to be enough. Thanks so much. Then there is the question of that case: I don't want to have to keep it for the rest of my life. I'll have it brought down to the hall, and you can pretend to be watching over it. Then I shall just leave quietly for the station. After about ten minutes, you can walk off to the smoking-room. The hotel will send round a note about the case later and then the owner can come for it.'

Jerton agreed to this. He watched over the case while the lady left the hotel. Her departure was not, however, completely unnoticed. Two gentlemen were standing near Jerton, and he heard one of them say to the other:

'Did you see that tall young woman in grey who went out just now? She is the Lady —'

But just as Jerton thought he was about to hear who she was, the men turned and walked away. Jerton thought it would not be well-mannered to run after them, break into their conversation, and ask for information concerning another person. Besides, he was supposed to be looking after the case. In a minute or two, however, the man who knew the young woman's name came walking back, alone. Jerton gathered up all his courage and called to him.

Mrs Stroope

'I think I heard you say you knew the lady who went out of the hotel a few minutes ago, the tall young lady, dressed in grey. Excuse me for asking, but could you tell me her name? I've been talking to her for half an hour; she … er … she seems to know me, so I suppose I've met her somewhere before. I just can't remember who she is. Could you — ?'

'Certainly. She's Mrs Stroope.'

'"Mrs?"' asked Jerton, surprised.

'Yes, she is the Lady Top Golfer where I live — quite a good golf player. She's a very nice person, and has a lot of Lord and Lady friends, but she has an awkward habit of losing her memory every now and then. It gets her into all sorts of trouble. She becomes very angry, too, if you say anything about it afterwards. Good day, sir.'

The stranger went on his way. Before Jerton had time to think about what he'd learned, he saw an angry-looking woman talking to the hotel porters in a loud and worried voice.

'Has any luggage been brought here from the station by mistake, with the name Kestrel-Smith? A small case — I can't find it anywhere. I saw it put on the train at Victoria Station, I am quite sure about that. Why — there it is! And look, the locks have been forced open!'

Jerton decided it was time he left. He walked hurriedly to the hotel garden, and sat out there for hours.

CLOVIS SANGRAIL AND FRIENDS

THE SURPRISING OF LADY BASTABLE

The bribe

'It would be rather nice if you would look after Clovis for another six days: I have to go to Scotland to visit the MacGregors',' said Mrs Sangrail sleepily across the breakfast-table. She always spoke in a sleepy, comfortable voice whenever she was unusually interested in something. It put people at their ease, and they frequently did what she wanted before they had realized that she was really asking for anything.

Lady Bastable, however, could not be tricked so easily. Possibly she knew her friend's special voice and what it was used for — at any rate, she knew Clovis.

She frowned at a piece of toast and ate it slowly, but did not offer to have Clovis in her home for six more days.

'It would help so much,' said Mrs Sangrail, giving up pretending she didn't really care. 'I especially don't want to take him to the MacGregors', and it will only be for six days.'

'It will seem longer,' said Lady Bastable unhappily. 'The last time he stayed here for a week —'

'I know,' interrupted the other quickly, 'but that was nearly two years ago. He was younger then.'

'But he hasn't improved,' said her hostess. 'It's no use growing older if you only learn new ways of misbehaving.'

Mrs Sangrail was unable to disagree. Since Clovis had reached the age of seventeen, she had never ceased to complain about his behaviour to all her closer friends. No one would have believed her if she had claimed he was improving.

She gave up trying to persuade her friend with words. She turned to bribery.

'If you'll have him here for these six days, I'll forget about the money you owe me from our last game of bridge.'

It was only forty-nine shillings, but Lady Bastable loved shillings with a great, strong love. To lose money at bridge and not to have to pay was one of those rare experiences of life that have to be enjoyed when they happen. It made card-playing especially attractive in her eyes.

Mrs Sangrail was almost equally in love with the money she had won. However, the possibility of finding a home for her son for six days, and saving his railway fare to Scotland, made the forgiving of Lady Bastable's debt seem worthwhile. When Clovis appeared at the breakfast-table, late as usual, everything had been agreed.

'Just think,' said Mrs Sangrail sleepily, 'Lady Bastable has very kindly asked you to stay here with her while I go to the MacGregors'.'

Clovis said all the right things in a highly incorrect way. He began to eat his breakfast with a black, angry look on his face. The arrangement between his mother and Lady Bastable had been made without anyone asking what he would like, and it was doubly displeasing to him. To begin with, he especially wanted to teach the MacGregor boys how to play poker-patience — a new card game he had learned. The second thing was that, although there was always plenty of food at the Bastable home, he did not like it.

Watching him from behind her sleepy-looking eyelids, his mother realized that it was too soon to feel any happiness over the success of her plan. Her long experience of Clovis told her that finding him somewhere to stay for a few days was one thing; getting him to stay there quietly and on his best behaviour was quite a different matter.

A debt repaid

Immediately after breakfast, Lady Bastable went to the morning-room and spent a quiet hour looking through the papers. She read them every day. Politics did not greatly interest her, but she had for many years been afraid that one day there would be a terrible revolution, in which everybody would be killed by everybody else. 'It will happen sooner than we think,' she would often remark mysteriously.

On this particular morning, the sight of Lady Bastable reading through her newspapers, searching for signs of social discontent, gave Clovis an idea. It was something his mind had been struggling towards all through breakfast time.

His mother had gone upstairs to get ready for her journey to Scotland, and he was alone downstairs with his hostess — and the servants. The servants were to play an important part in his plan. At this time of the morning, Clovis knew they would all be in the kitchen area, enjoying a mid-morning cup of tea, and receiving their orders for the rest of the day from the butler.

Clovis ran to the kitchen. Without knocking first, he threw open the door and screamed out wildly: 'Poor Lady Bastable! In the morning-room! Oh, quickly! Quickly!'

The next moment, the cook, two or three maids, the butler and a gardener, who had all happened to be in the kitchen, were following after Clovis as he rushed back towards the morning-room.

Lady Bastable's reading of the newspapers was interrupted when she heard a loud crash in the hall. It sounded as if a piece of furniture, a chair, or the Japanese screen, had been knocked down. Then the door leading from the hall flew open. Her young guest ran madly through the room. As he went past her, he shouted, 'The revolution! They're after us!' He crossed the room and, as quick as lightning, shot through the open French windows into the gardens.

The next moment, a crowd of servants burst into the morning-room with very serious looks on their faces. The gardener was still holding the knife with which he had been cutting back the hedges earlier that morning.

In their hurry to reach Lady Bastable, they all began slipping and sliding as they crossed the smooth polished floor. They pushed into one another, as if fighting to be first to reach the chair where their mistress sat in horrified amazement.

If she had had just a moment to think about what might be happening, she would have behaved, as she afterwards explained, much more calmly. It was probably the gardener's knife that convinced her. She followed Clovis through the French windows, and ran well and far across the garden before the eyes of her astonished servants.

A calm, orderly atmosphere is not something which can be restored immediately: both Lady Bastable and the butler found the process of returning to normal conditions extremely difficult. Having servants running through the house, even when it occurs for the best of reasons, cannot fail to leave some small feelings of embarrassment behind. By lunch-time, however, everything had calmed down, and the meal was served in a very quiet fashion, that was a model of respectable behaviour. Half-way through, the butler presented Mrs Sangrail with an envelope lying on a silver tray. It contained a cheque for forty-nine shillings.

The MacGregor boys learned how to play poker-patience that summer; and Clovis found the food in Scotland very much to his liking.

The Letters

A perfect spring afternoon

On a late spring afternoon Ella McCarthy sat on a green-painted chair in Kensington Gardens. She was clearly waiting for someone.

'Hello, Bertie!' she exclaimed, when her boyfriend finally arrived and sat down on the chair nearest to her own, 'Hasn't it been a perfect spring afternoon?'

The statement was completely untrue as far as Ella's own feelings were concerned; until the arrival of Bertie, the afternoon had been terrible.

Bertie made a suitable reply, and seemed to be asking something at the same time.

'Thank you so very much for those lovely handkerchiefs,' said Ella, answering the unspoken question. 'They were just what I wanted. But there's only one thing that makes me unhappy about your gift,' she added, with a frown.

'What is that?' said Bertie anxiously, fearing that perhaps he had chosen a size of handkerchief that was not correct for presentation to a young lady.

'I should have liked to have written and thanked you for them as soon as I got them,' said Ella.

'But you know how my mother is,' Bertie protested. 'She opens all my letters. If she found I'd been giving presents to anyone, she'd have talked about it for two weeks at least.'

'Surely, at the age of twenty —' began Ella.

'I'm not twenty till September,' interrupted Bertie.

'At nineteen years and eight months,' Ella continued, 'you might be allowed to keep your letters to yourself.'

'I ought to be, but things aren't always what they ought to be. Mother opens every letter that comes into the house, whoever it's for. My sisters and I have argued with her about it time and again, but she goes on doing it.'

'I'd find some way to stop her if I were you,' said Ella.

Bertie felt that the wonderful qualities of his carefully chosen present were fading away.

Not a joking matter

'Is anything the matter?' asked Bertie's friend, Clovis, when they met that evening at the swimming-pool.

'Why do you ask?' said Bertie.

'When you wear such a look of great unhappiness in a swimming-pool,' said Clovis, 'it's especially clear. After all, you're wearing very little else at the time. Didn't Ella like the handkerchiefs?'

Bertie explained the situation.

'It is rather upsetting, you know,' he added, 'when a girl has a lot of things she wants to write to you but can't send a letter.'

'You're luckier than you realize,' said Clovis. 'I have to spend a good amount of time making excuses for not writing back to people.'

'It's not a joking matter,' said Bertie. 'You wouldn't find it funny if your mother opened all your letters.'

'The funny thing to me is that you should let her do it.'

'I can't stop her. I've argued about it —'

'You haven't used the right kind of argument, I'm sure. Now, if every time one of your letters was opened, you lay on your back on the table during dinner-time and had a fit, or woke the entire family in the middle of the night to recite one of Blake's "Poems of Innocence", you might succeed. People think more about an upset meal or a broken night's rest, than a broken heart.'

'Oh, you're no help!' said Bertie angrily, splashing Clovis from head to foot as he dived into the water.

The letters

A day or two after the conversation in the swimming-pool, a letter addressed to Bertie Heasant slid into the letter-box at his home. It then slid into the hands of his mother.

Mrs Heasant was one of those empty-minded persons to whom other people's affairs are the most interesting thing in life. The more private they are, the more interesting they seem. She would have opened the letter in any case, but the fact that it was marked 'private', and smelled of scent, caused her to open it in a greater hurry than usual. What she saw was more amazing then she'd ever thought possible:

'Bertie, dearest,' it began, 'I wonder if you will be brave enough to do it; and you must be very brave, too. Don't forget the jewels. They are a detail but details interest me.

Yours as ever,
CLOTILDE

P.S. Your mother must not know about me. If asked, swear you never heard of me.'

For years Mrs Heasant had searched Bertie's letters for hints of possible wrong-doing or youthful love affairs. At last all her suspicions were proved right by this one amazing letter. That any one with the foreign-sounding name 'Clotilde' should send a letter to Bertie using words like 'as ever' was strange enough. The remark about the jewels was even stranger, and quite shocking. Mrs Heasant could think of books and plays in which jewels had been important. Here, under her own roof, before her very eyes, her own son was receiving letters from a woman to whom jewels were just an interesting detail.

Bertie was not going to be home for another hour, but his sisters were at home and Mrs Heasant screamed to them, 'Bertie is being used by some evil woman. Her name is Clotilde.' She thought they had better know the worst at once.

By the time Bertie arrived, his mother had discussed every possible and impossible explanation for his guilty secret; the girls held the opinion that their brother had been weak, rather than wicked.

'Who is Clotilde?' was the question that hit Bertie almost before he had got into the hall. When he declared he knew no one by that name, his mother laughed bitterly.

'How obedient you are to her!' she exclaimed. But she soon grew quite angry when she realized that Bertie did not intend to make things any clearer.

'You shan't have any dinner till you've told me everything,' she said loudly. Bertie said nothing. He quickly gathered some food from the kitchen and locked himself in his bedroom.

His mother made frequent visits to the locked door. There she shouted a series of questions as though she thought that if you ask a question often enough and loudly enough, an answer will come.

An hour had passed in this way when another letter addressed to Bertie and marked 'private' appeared in the letter-box. Mrs Heasant jumped on it like a cat that has missed the first mouse, and then unexpectedly sees a second.

'So you have really done it!' the letter began. *'Poor Dagmar. Now that she is dead I almost pity her. You did it very well, you evil boy. The servants all think she killed herself and no one suspects you. Better not touch the jewels till after the funeral.*

CLOTILDE'

Mrs Heasant raced upstairs and beat furiously at her son's door.

'Terrible boy, what have you done to Dagmar?'

'It's Dagmar now, is it?' Bertie snapped. 'I suppose it will be Geraldine next.'

'That this should happen, after all my efforts to keep you at home in the evening,' cried Mrs Heasant. 'It's no use trying to hide things from me — Clotilde's letter tells everything.'

'Does it tell who she is?' asked Bertie. 'I've heard so much about her, I should like to know something about her home life. Seriously, if you go on like this, I shall have to fetch a doctor. You've often screamed at me about nothing, but I've never heard you drag all sorts of imaginary women into the discussion.'

'Are these letters imaginary?' screamed Mrs Heasant. 'What about the jewels? What about Dagmar, and why did you kill her?'

'I would have known'

Bertie made no attempt to offer a solution to these problems. However, the last post of the evening brought another letter for him. Its contents told Mrs Heasant what her son had already worked out.

> *'Dear Bertie,' it said, 'I hope I haven't made you upset with the letters I've been sending under the name of "Clotilde". You told me the other day that the servants, or somebody at your home, opened your letters. So I thought I would give anyone that opened them something exciting to read. The shock might do them good.*
>
> *Yours,*
> *CLOVIS SANGRAIL'*

Mrs Heasant knew Clovis slightly, and was rather afraid of him. It was not difficult to see at whom the joke was aimed. In a quieter mood she knocked once more at Bertie's door.

'A letter from Mr Sangrail. It's all been a stupid joke. He wrote those other letters. Why, where are you going?'

Bertie had opened the bedroom door; he had on his hat and overcoat.

'I'm going to get the doctor. I want him to come and see if anything's the matter with you. Of course it was all a joke — no person in his right mind could have believed all that nonsense about murder and jewels. You've been making enough noise to bring the house down for the last hour or two.'

'But what was I to think of those letters?' said Mrs Heasant.

'I would have known what to think of them,' said Bertie. 'I would have seen they were just one of Clovis's jokes. If you choose to excite yourself over other people's letters, it's your own fault. Anyhow, I'm going for the doctor.'

It was Bertie's great opportunity, and he knew it. His mother knew that she would look rather foolish if people heard about what had happened.

'I'll never open your letters again,' she promised.

And Clovis has no better friend than Bertie Heasant.

THE RESCUE

The gambler

Rex Dillot was nearly twenty-four, almost good-looking, and quite poor. His mother gave him what money she could spare, and Rex occasionally earned money as a secretary or companion to people who needed help.

Still, Rex lived fairly comfortably. He was quite clever at it, and with the help of Good Luck, or Fate, his weekend invitations seemed to arrive on the days when his only good suit of clothes had just come back from the cleaners.

He played most games badly, and was clever enough to know this, but he had developed a wonderful ability to judge the skill of other people, whether in a golf match, at billiards, or whatever. By giving his opinion that a certain player would surely win, he usually succeeded in making bets that he won. He made enough money this way at the weekends to pay for his living expenses for the rest of the week.

The trouble was, as he said to Clovis Sangrail, he never had much money to place on a bet, and so he never won really large amounts.

A safe bet

'Some day,' he said, 'I shall come across a really safe thing, a bet that simply can't go wrong, and then I shall bet everything I have, or even a good deal more.'

'It would be awkward if you didn't win,' said Clovis.

'It would be more than awkward,' said Rex, 'it would be a tragedy. All the same, it would be extremely amusing if I won. Imagine waking up one morning with a small fortune you didn't have the day before. I would be in such a good mood that I would clean out all my hostess's bird cages before breakfast.'

'Your hostess might not have any bird cages,' said Clovis.

'I always choose hostesses that have,' said Rex. 'Only women with open, generous characters keep birds. I like people who spend time throwing seed at a lot of silly little feathered things that do nothing but sing and look at each other. That kind of person is sure to be nice to humans as well.'

'Young Strinnit is coming down this afternoon,' said Clovis thoughtfully. 'You won't find it difficult to get him to bet on himself at a game of billiards. He plays well, but he's not quite as good as he thinks.'

'I know one member of the party who can beat him,' said Rex softly, 'that Major who arrived last night. I've seen him play at St Moritz. If I could get Strinnit to bet on himself against the Major, the money would be safe in my pocket. This looks like the good thing I've been watching and praying for.'

'Take care,' advised Clovis. 'The Major may not always play that well.'

'If I am always careful, I shall never be rich,' said Rex quietly to himself.

A silly game

'Are you all going to rush off to the billiard-room?' asked Teresa Thundleford, after dinner. She clearly disapproved of this plan. 'I can't see the fun in watching two men playing with coloured balls on a green table.'

'Oh, well,' said her hostess, 'it's a way of passing the time.'

'A very poor way, in my opinion,' said Mrs Thundleford. 'I was going to show all of you the photographs I took in Venice last summer.'

'You showed them to us last night,' said her hostess quickly.

'Last night I showed you the ones I took in Florence. These are quite a different lot.'

'Oh, well, some time tomorrow we can look at them. Why don't you leave them on a table downstairs, and then everyone can have a look whenever they wish.'

'I prefer to show them when we are all gathered together, as I have quite a lot to explain about Venetian art. Also, there are some poems of mine that I should like to read to you. But, of course, if you all prefer to watch Major Latton and Mr Strinnit knocking balls about on a table —'

'They are both excellent players,' said the hostess.

'I hope you don't mean that my poems and my art talks are less than excellent,' said Mrs Thundleford coldly. 'However, as you all seem to want to watch a silly game, there's no more to be said. I shall go upstairs and finish some writing. Later on, perhaps, I will come down and join you.'

Disgrace

To one, at least, of the watchers, the game was not at all silly. It was exciting, upsetting and finally it grew to be tragic. The Major was not playing as well as expected, and young Strinnit was playing better than ever. Strinnit had all the luck of the game as well.

'A hundred and seventy to seventy-four,' sang out the youth who was keeping score. The first person to get two hundred and fifty points would win. Strinnit was clearly well ahead. Clovis saw the excitement die away from Dillot's face, and a hard, white look take its place.

'How much money have you bet?' whispered Clovis. The other whispered the amount through dry, shaking lips. It was more than he or any one he knew could pay; he had done what he said he would do. He had been very careless.

'Two hundred and six to ninety-eight.'

Rex heard a clock strike ten somewhere in the hall, then another somewhere else, and another, and another — the house seemed full of striking clocks. In another hour they would all be striking eleven, and he would be listening to them in disgrace, unable to pay, even in part, the bet he had made.

'Two hundred and eighteen, to one hundred and three.' The game was nearly over. Rex hoped that the ceiling would fall down, or the house would catch fire. He hoped for anything that would stop that horrible rolling of red and white balls.

'Two hundred and twenty-eight, to one hundred and seven.'

The rescuer

Rex opened his cigarette-case; it was empty. That at least gave him an excuse to leave the room. He would not have to watch the hopeless game played out to the finish. He walked up a short stairway to a long, silent hall of bedrooms, each with a guest's name written on a little square card pinned to the door. In the silence he could still hear the terrible click-click of the balls coming from the billiard-room. If he waited for a few minutes longer, he would hear the loud clapping and congratulations that would follow Strinnit's victory.

Suddenly he became aware of another sound, the noisy, angry breathing of someone in a heavy after-dinner sleep. The sound came from a room close by. The door was slightly open, and the name written on the little square card said, 'Mrs Thundleford.' Rex pushed the door open an inch or two more and looked in.

Teresa Thundleford had fallen asleep over a book on Italian art. At her side, somewhat dangerously near the edge of the table, was an oil lamp. If Fate had been kind to him, thought Rex, bitterly, that lamp would have been knocked over by the sleeper: it would have started a fire, and given them all something to think of besides billiards.

There are times when one must take Fate in one's own hands. Rex took the lamp in his.

'Two hundred and thirty-seven, to one hundred and fifteen.' Strinnit was at the table, and the balls lay in a good position for him; he had a choice of two fairly easy shots, a choice which he was never to decide.

A sudden storm of screams and a rush of feet sent everyone running to the door. Rex Dillot crashed into the room, carrying in his arms the loudly-screaming Teresa Thundleford. Her clothing was certainly not all in flames but the edge of her skirt was burning a little, as well as part of the tablecloth in which Rex had wrapped her. Rex threw her on to the billiard-table, and for one minute, the work of beating out the weak flames with rugs and cushions, and soda-water kept everyone busy.

'It was lucky I was passing when it happened,' exclaimed Rex. 'Some one had better see to the room — I think the rug is on fire up there.'

As a matter of fact, the quickness and energy of the rescuer had prevented any great damage being done, either to Mrs Thundleford or to her room. The billiard-table was ruined, however, and had to be repaired. Perhaps it was not the best place on which to have put the woman down; but then, as Clovis said, when one is rushing about with a burning woman in one's arms, one doesn't stop to think out exactly where to put her.

3

THE HOUNDS OF FATE

Tired and hungry

It was a dull autumn afternoon, and getting dark. Martin Stoner walked slowly, and with some difficulty, along a muddy lane. He had no idea exactly where he was going. Somewhere in front of him, he believed, lay the sea, and that seemed to be the direction his legs wanted to take him. Why he was struggling wearily forward to that goal he could scarcely have explained, unless it was something to do with the way hunted animals, in their fear, sometimes run towards the sea. In his case the hounds of fate, those dogs that hunt us through our lives, were close behind him. Weariness and hopelessness, and the cold, damp weather had almost beaten him. He hardly knew what he was doing: he did not know where he was going, and did not care.

Stoner was one of those unfortunate people who seem to have tried everything, but succeeded in nothing. Now his life seemed to be coming to an end. He was out of money and out of ideas — there was nothing more to try.

Unlike some other men, his difficulties had not forced him to find new strength and the energy to start again. As Stoner's fortunes went from bad to worse, he found it more and more difficult to think of a way out of them. With the clothes he stood up in, a few pennies in his pocket, and not a single friend to ask for help, with no arrangements made to stay anywhere, Martin Stoner struggled steadily forward. He walked wearily between hedges and beneath trees that were damp with a heavy mist that was turning to rain. His mind was almost a blank, except that he was vaguely aware that somewhere in front of him lay the sea.

Something else began to work through to his mind now and then — the knowledge that he was miserably hungry. Presently he stopped by an open gateway that led into a large farm-garden. There were not many signs of life here, and the farmhouse at the further end of the garden looked cold and unfriendly. It was beginning to rain more heavily, however, and Stoner thought that here, perhaps, he might obtain shelter for a few minutes, and buy a glass of milk with his last few coins.

He turned wearily into the garden and followed a narrow path up to a side door. Before he had time to knock, the door opened and a thin, bent old man stood to one side in the doorway, as though to let him pass through.

'Could I come in out of the rain?' Stoner began, but the old man interrupted him.

'Come in, Master Tom. I knew you would come back one of these days.'

Stoner stepped into the farmhouse and stood staring at the other: he did not understand.

'Sit down while I get some supper for you,' said the old man, who seemed happy to see him.

A night's shelter

Stoner's legs gave way from weariness as he sank weakly into the armchair that had been pushed up to him. In another minute he was eating cold meat, cheese and bread, which had been placed on the small table at his side.

'You've not changed much over the past four years,' went on the old man, in a voice that to Stoner sounded far away, like something in a dream, 'but you'll find we have changed. It's not like it was when you left. There are not many of us left: only me and your old Aunt are living here now. I'll go and tell her that you've come. She won't want to see you, I don't suppose, but she'll let you stay. She always said if you came back you could stay, but she wouldn't ever want to set eyes on you or speak to you again.'

The old man placed a mug of beer on the table beside Stoner and then went slowly away down a long passage.

The rain had now changed to a furious storm, which beat noisily against door and windows. Stoner thought with a shudder of what the sea-shore must look like in such weather as this, with night coming on. He finished the food and the beer and sat waiting for the return of his strange host. As the minutes ticked by on the clock in the corner of the room, a new hope began to grow in the young man's mind; it was an enlargement of his former longing for food and a few minutes' rest. He began to hope, now, that he might be given a night's shelter in this house, which seemed so strangely hospitable. There was a noise of footsteps down the passage as the farm servant returned.

'The old Missus won't see you, Master Tom, but she says you can stay. That's fair enough: the farm will be yours when she is dead and in her grave. I've had a fire lit in your old room, Master Tom, and the maid has put fresh sheets on the bed. You'll find nothing changed up there. Perhaps you're feeling tired and would like to go to your room now.'

Without a word Martin Stoner got slowly to his feet and followed the old man along a passage, up a short, narrow staircase, along another passage, and into a large room lit with a cheerfully blazing fire. There was only a little furniture. It was plain and old-fashioned, but good of its kind. He also noticed a stuffed animal in a glass case and a picture on the wall. But Stoner was interested only in the bed. He could scarcely wait to tear his clothes off before rolling, in a luxury of weariness, into its comfortable depths. The hounds of fate seemed to have stopped worrying him for a while.

Master Tom

In the cold light of morning, Stoner laughed quietly to himself as he slowly remembered where he was and the position he was in. It wasn't a happy laugh. Everything that ever happened to him went wrong in the end, and he did not expect this to be any different. But perhaps, as he looked so much like this missing 'Tom', who clearly was a man with a bad reputation, he might be given some breakfast. After that he would get safely away before anyone discovered the truth.

The Hounds of Fate

In the room downstairs, he found the old man ready with a dish of bacon and fried eggs for 'Master Tom's' breakfast. The maid, a hard-faced elderly woman, brought in a teapot and poured him out a cup of tea. As he sat at the table, a small, brown-coloured dog — a spaniel — came up to him in a friendly way.

'That's old Bowker's pup,' explained the old man, whom the maid had called George. 'She loved you, that old dog did; she was never the same after you went away to Australia. She died about a year ago. That's her pup.'

Stoner found it difficult to feel sad about the death of a dog he had never known — and one who would have quickly made it clear he was not the 'Master Tom' she loved so well.

'You'll go for a ride, Master Tom?' was the next surprising suggestion that came from the old man. 'We've a nice two-year-old that's a strong, fast little horse. Old Biddy is getting a bit slow now, though she is still a good animal, but I'll have the two-year-old got ready for you and brought round to the door.'

'I've got nothing to wear for horse-riding,' said Stoner, almost laughing as he looked down at his one suit of well-worn clothes.

'Master Tom,' said the old man, almost as if his feelings had been hurt, 'all your things are just as you left them. We'll put them in front of the fire for a while, to get the damp out of them, and then they'll be all right. A little riding and some shooting now and then will help you pass the time. You'll need it. You don't have any friends round here, you know. They all hate you still, and haven't forgotten or forgiven anything. No one will want to have anything to do with you, so you had better get what enjoyment you can from horse and dog. They're good company, too.'

Old George went away to give his orders, and Stoner, feeling more than ever as if he were in a dream, went upstairs to look through 'Master Tom's' clothes. A ride was one of the pleasures dearest to his heart, and he felt safer knowing that none of Tom's previous friends would want to meet him.

The decision

The clothes fitted quite well, and as he was getting into them, he wondered what the real Tom had done to set everyone against him. However, the sound of quick, eager hoofs on damp earth stopped that line of thought for the moment. The two-year-old had been brought to the side door, and was waiting impatiently for him.

'I'm a beggar on a horse,' thought Stoner to himself, as he rode swiftly along the muddy lanes through which he had struggled the day before. Then he stopped thinking about the unhappiness of his life and gave himself up to the pleasure of a fast ride along a flat stretch of country road.

At an open gateway he slowed down to let two farm-carts turn into a field. The lads driving the carts found time to give him a long stare. As he passed on, he heard an excited voice call out, 'It's Tom Prike! So he's come back here again, has he?' The likeness, which had convinced an old man close up, was clearly good enough to mislead younger eyes at a short distance.

During his ride he soon noticed that local folk had neither forgotten nor forgiven the crime which the absent Tom had passed on to him. Black, angry looks, muttering, and whispering greeted him whenever he rode past any groups of people. 'Bowker's pup,' running contentedly by his side, seemed the one friendly creature in a very unfriendly world.

Back at the farmhouse, as he was getting off the horse at the side door, he caught a glimpse of an elderly woman peering at him from behind the curtain of an upper window. This, he thought, must be his newly-acquired aunt.

Over the midday meal that was on the table waiting for him, Stoner was able to think about the possibilities of his strange situation. The real Tom, after four years of absence, might suddenly arrive at the farm, or a letter might come from him at any moment. Again, as heir to the farm, the false Tom might be asked to sign documents, and that would be highly embarrassing. Or a relative might arrive who, unlike the aunt, would want to see him. All these things would mean the truth would come out.

On the other hand, there was the open sky, the cold, the rain, and the muddy lanes that led down to the sea. The farm offered him, at any rate, a temporary shelter from total poverty; farming was one of the many things he had 'tried,' and he would be able to do a certain amount of work in return for the hospitality that he was enjoying.

'Will you have cold pork for your supper,' asked the hard-faced maid, as she cleared the table, 'or will you have it heated up?'

'Hot, with plenty of onions,' said Stoner. It was the only time in his life that he had made a quick decision. And as he gave the order, he knew that he meant to stay.

A sad business

Stoner never attempted to wander about the house. He only used those rooms which Old George had shown him — where he slept and ate. When he took part in the farm-work, it was as one who worked under orders. He never told anyone what to do. Old George, the two-year-old, and Bowker's pup were his only companions in a world that was otherwise cold and unfriendly.

Of the mistress of the farm he saw nothing. Once, when he knew she had gone to church, he made a quick visit to the sitting-room in an attempt to find out what he could about the young man whose place he had taken, and whose bad reputation he had accepted as his own. There were many photographs hung on the walls, or stuck in frames, but there were none of the young man. At last, in an album hidden at the back of a bookshelf, he discovered what he wanted. As he turned the pages, he found a whole series, labelled 'Tom.' There was a small, fat child of three; an awkward boy of about twelve; a rather good-looking lad of sixteen with very smooth, carefully parted hair, and, finally, a young man in his early twenties. At this last photograph Stoner looked with particular interest; anyone would agree that he and the young man in the photograph looked very much alike.

From the lips of Old George, who had plenty to say on most subjects, he tried again and again to learn something about what 'Master Tom' had done to make everyone avoid and hate him.

'What do the people around here say about me?' he asked one day as they were walking home from a field they had been working in.

The old man shook his head.

'They are very angry with you, Master Tom, extraordinarily angry. It's a sad business, it certainly is; it's a very sad business.'

And nothing would ever persuade the old man to say anything more than that.

'You must get away from here'

On a clear, cold evening, a few days before Christmas, Stoner stood in a corner of the orchard from which he had a wide view of the countryside. Here and there he could see dots of light coming from lamps or candles in homes where people were enjoying all the family warmth and happiness of the season. Behind him lay the grey, silent farmhouse, where no one ever laughed and little was said. Even a quarrel, there, would have made a pleasant change.

As he turned to look at the long, dark front of the building, a door opened and Old George came out. He seemed to be in a great hurry. Stoner heard him call out the name he had adopted. The old man seemed to be worried about something.

Instantly Stoner knew that something had happened. Suddenly his thoughts changed. This house, cold and silent as it was, was also a place of peace and contentment. He hated the thought of having to leave it.

'Master Tom,' said the old man in a whisper, 'you must get away from here for a few days. Michael Ley is back in the village. He swears he will shoot you if he can find you. He'll do it, too. There's murder in his eyes. Get away tonight, while it's dark. You need only stay away for a week or two. He won't be here any longer than that.'

'But where shall I go?' said Stoner. The old man was obviously terrified, and Stoner began to feel frightened, too.

'Go along the coast as far as you can, to Punchford, and stay hidden there. When Michael's gone, I'll ride the two-year-old over to the Green Dragon Inn; when you see it there, you will know that it is all right for you to come back again.'

'But —' began Stoner, uncertain how he was going to manage — he was as poor as the day he arrived.

'You don't need to worry about the cost,' said the other. 'The old Missus agrees you had better go, and she asked me to give you this.'

The old man handed over three gold sovereigns and a few shillings — an amount that would have paid Stoner's expenses for a month or more.

His old self again

Stoner felt more of a cheat than ever, as he walked quickly away that night with the old woman's money in his pocket. Old George and Bowker's pup stood watching him silently from the yard. He found it difficult to believe that he would ever come back, and he felt sad to think of those two simple friends who would wait hopefully for his return. Some day perhaps, the real Tom would come back, and then there would be much discussion about the identity of the mysterious guest they had welcomed under their roof.

He was not greatly worried about his own fate. He knew it was not possible to live for very long in this world on three sovereigns, but to a man who was used to thinking himself lucky if he had a few pennies to spend, it seemed a good start. In a rather strange way, fortune had been kind to him when he last walked down these lanes as a hopeless wanderer. Now there might still be a chance of his finding some work and beginning his life all over again.

As he got further from the farm, his feelings grew lighter and more hopeful. There was a sense of relief at being his old self again, and ceasing to act the uneasy part of another man. He gave no thought to the enemy who had so suddenly dropped into his life. Since his life as Master Tom was now behind him, Master Tom's enemies were not for him to worry about. For the first time for many months, he began to hum a light-hearted little tune to himself.

Then there stepped out from the shadow of a large, old tree a man with a gun. There was no need to wonder who he might be. The moonlight falling on his white face showed a look of human hate far greater than Stoner in all his wandering about the world had ever seen before. Stoner jumped to one side. He made a wild effort to break through the hedge at the side of the lane, but he could not force a way through the tough branches. The hounds of fate had waited for him in those narrow lanes. This time he would not be able to avoid them.

Wild Boys

Laura

Life after death

'You are not really dying, are you?' asked Amanda

'The doctor says I will die by Tuesday,' said Laura.

'But today is Saturday. This is serious!' gasped Amanda.

'I don't know about it being serious; it is certainly Saturday,' said Laura.

'Death is always serious,' said Amanda.

'I never said I was going to die. I am going to stop being Laura, but I shall go on being something. An animal of some kind, I suppose. You see, when one hasn't been very good in the life one has just lived, one returns to life as some lower animal. And I haven't been very good really. I've been bad-mannered and mean and revengeful — but of course, only when people have seemed to deserve it.'

'People never deserve that sort of thing,' said Amanda quickly.

'If you don't mind my saying so,' answered Laura, 'Egbert is a person who deserves plenty of that sort of thing. You're married to him — that's different. You have to love, honour, and be patient with him: I don't.'

'There's nothing wrong with Egbert,' protested Amanda.

'Oh, I know. I am the one who is wrong,' admitted Laura without really feeling it. 'Egbert is just the reason why I have done so many bad things. He became so angry, for instance, when I took the dogs for a walk the other day.'

'They chased his best chickens, stopped two hens from laying eggs, and then ran all over the flower beds. You know how much he loves his chickens and his garden.'

'Anyhow, he needn't have complained about it for the whole evening and said, "Let's not talk about it any more" just when I was enjoying the discussion. That's when I decided on revenge,' added Laura. She laughed without showing the least amount of sorrow. 'I drove the entire family of chickens into his garden shed the next morning.'

'How could you do such a thing?' exclaimed Amanda.

'It was quite easy,' said Laura. 'Another two hens were trying to lay eggs at the time, but I made them understand I wanted them to move.'

'And we thought it was an accident!'

'You see,' continued Laura, 'I really have good reason for thinking that I shall be a lower animal in my next life. But I haven't been that terrible, so I expect to be a nice animal, something lively, and full of fun. An otter, perhaps.'

'I can't imagine you as an otter,' said Amanda.

'Well, I don't suppose you can imagine me as an angel, either,' said Laura.

Amanda was silent. She couldn't.

'Personally I think an otter's life would be rather pleasant,' continued Laura. 'Fresh fish to eat all the year round, and a wonderfully beautiful, slim, strong body.'

'Think of the dogs that hunt otters,' said Amanda. 'How terrible to be hunted and chased and finally bitten to death!'

'Oh, not so bad, with all the neighbourhood watching and admiring you for your courage as you fight back. It is no worse than a slow death from Saturday to Tuesday. Anyway, then I should go on to something else. If I had been a fairly good otter, I suppose I should get back into a human shape of some sort; probably something rather uncivilized — a wild, little jungle boy, I should think.'

'I wish you would be serious,' sighed Amanda. 'You really ought to be if you're only going to live till Tuesday.'

The otter

As a matter of fact, Laura died on Monday.

'So very inconvenient,' Amanda complained to her uncle Sir Lulworth Quayne. 'I asked quite a lot of people down for golf and fishing. Why did she choose today to die?'

'Laura always was making difficulties,' said Sir Lulworth. 'She was born at Easter time: we had a woman staying in the house then who hated babies.'

'She had an idea that she was going to return to life as an otter,' said Amanda.

'One meets with those ideas so frequently nowadays, even in the West,' said Sir Lulworth. 'There may be some truth in them, I suppose. Laura was such an unusual person in this life that anything could happen.'

'You think she really might have passed into some animal form?' asked Amanda. She was one of those people who mould their opinions rather quickly on the ideas of those around them.

Just then Egbert entered the room. He was looking very unhappy, but not because of Laura's death.

'Four of my best hens have been killed,' he exclaimed. 'One of them was dragged away and eaten right in the middle of the new plants that I've been working so hard on. My best flowers and my best hens — it almost seems as if the animal knew exactly how to cause the greatest damage.'

'Was it a fox, do you think?' asked Amanda.

'Sounds more like a wild cat,' said Sir Lulworth.

'No,' said Egbert, 'there were footprints all over the place, and we followed the tracks down to the stream at the bottom of the garden; it was definitely an otter.'

Amanda looked quickly and secretly at Sir Lulworth. Egbert was too upset to eat any breakfast. He went out to fix the fence round the chicken yard.

'I think she might at least have waited till the funeral was over,' said Amanda in a shocked voice.

'It's her own funeral, you know,' said Sir Lulworth. 'It's hard to say how much respect one should show — at one's own death.'

Disrespect for the recently dead was taken to further lengths the next day. While the family was away from the house, at the funeral, the rest of the hens were killed. The murderer had gone straight through the flowers, and had also attacked the strawberry plants in the lower garden.

'I shall get the hunting dogs at the earliest possible moment,' said Egbert wildly.

'Oh no! You can't possibly do such a thing!' exclaimed Amanda. 'I mean,' she added quickly, 'it wouldn't be right, so soon after the funeral.'

'It's absolutely necessary,' said Egbert. 'Once an otter starts killing chickens, it will never stop.'

'Perhaps it will go somewhere else now that there are no hens left,' suggested Amanda.

'It sounds as though you want to protect that animal,' said Egbert.

'There's been so little water in the stream lately,' replied
15 Amanda, 'it hardly seems fair to hunt an animal when it has so little chance of escaping.'

'Good God!' said Egbert angrily. 'I'm not thinking about fairness. I want to have the animal killed as soon as possible.'

Even Amanda's opposition weakened when, during
20 church on the following Sunday, the otter got into the house, took half a fish from the ice box and ate it on the valuable Persian carpet in Egbert's room.

'It will be hiding under our beds and biting pieces out of our feet before long,' said Egbert. From what Amanda knew
25 of this particular otter, she felt that this was not impossible.

The little beast

It was Amanda's friend and neighbour, Aurora Burret, who brought Amanda news of the day's hunt.

'It's too bad you weren't with us — we had quite a good
30 day. We found it in the pool just below your garden.'

'Did you — kill it?' asked Amanda.

'Of course. A fine she-otter: a very slim, beautiful animal. Your husband got rather badly bitten trying to catch it. Poor thing, I felt quite sorry for it, it had such a human look in its eyes when it was killed. You'll call me silly, but do you know who that look reminded me of? Oh, my dear woman, what is the matter?'

Amanda had a nervous breakdown and was in hospital for a month. When she recovered, Egbert took her to Egypt for a quiet holiday.

The rest speedily brought her back to health and mental balance, and it was not long before the adventures of a hungry otter searching for food were seen as being nothing out of the ordinary. Amanda became her calm, old self again. Even the noise of angry shouting, coming from her husband's dressing-room, in her husband's voice, failed to disturb her as she sat reading one evening in a Cairo hotel.

'What is the matter? What has happened?' she asked with amused curiosity.

'That little beast! He has thrown all my clean shirts into the bath! You wait till I catch you, you little —'

'What little beast?' asked Amanda, trying not to laugh.

'This wild, little jungle boy, here in my room,' cried Egbert.

And now Amanda is seriously ill.

GABRIEL-ERNEST

Imagination

'There is a wild animal in your woods,' said Cunningham, as he was being driven to the station. It was the only remark he had made during the drive.

'There's a fox or two, perhaps, that may have wandered in, and some otters that live there. Nothing worse than that,' said Van Cheele. The artist said nothing.

'What did you mean about a wild animal?' said Van Cheele later, when they were at the station.

'Nothing. Just my imagination I expect. Here is the train,' said Cunningham.

That afternoon Van Cheele went for a long walk in the woodland which was part of his property. He knew the names of quite a number of birds and wild flowers there, so his aunt was possibly right when she described him as a great nature-lover. At any rate, he was a great walker.

When he was out on his walks, he made mental notes of everything he saw. He did not do this so much for scientific reasons: it was more for something to talk about when he got home. When the bluebells began to show themselves in flower, he made a point of telling everyone about it. The fact that it was spring, and everyone knew bluebells come into flower in spring should have made such an observation unnecessary. But at least they felt that he was being completely honest with them.

Tiger's eyes

What Van Cheele saw on this particular afternoon was, however, something he had never come across before. On a large, smooth rock overhanging a deep pool, which was surrounded by dark, old trees, a boy of about sixteen lay, drying his wet brown limbs in the sun. His wet hair lay close to his head. His light-brown eyes, so light that they almost looked like the eyes of a wild tiger, were turned towards Van Cheele with a certain lazy watchfulness. It was an unexpected sight, and Van Cheele found himself doing something he could not remember doing before. He was thinking before he spoke. Where on earth could this wild-looking boy come from?

The miller's wife had lost a boy some two months ago. Everyone thought he had been swept away by the river, which was then in flood, but that child had been a mere baby, not an almost fully-grown lad.

'What are you doing there?' he demanded.

'Can't you see? I am lying in the sun drying myself,' replied the boy.

'Where do you live?'

'Here, in these woods.'

'You can't live in the woods,' said Van Cheele.

'They are very nice woods,' said the boy, in a voice that suggested it must be perfectly obvious.

'But where do you sleep at night?'

'I don't sleep at night; that's when I am up and awake, and very busy.'

Van Cheele began to feel annoyed. How was it he did not seem to be able to understand the boy's answers?

'But what do you live on?' he asked.

'Meat,' said the boy, and he pronounced the word with pleasure, as though he were tasting it.

'Meat! What meat?'

'I don't know why you should want to know, but I'll tell you anyway: rabbits, wild birds, hares, chickens, lambs in the spring, children when I can get any; they're usually too well locked in at night, when I do most of my hunting. It's quite two months since I tasted child-meat.'

An extraordinary creature

Ignoring the last remark, Van Cheele tried to discover if the boy had been breaking any property laws. You could not just catch people's chickens and eat them, or even the hares that lived wild in the woods.

'You're talking nonsense when you say you eat hares' meat. The hares round here aren't at all easy to catch.'

'At night I hunt on four feet,' was the somewhat puzzling reply.

'I suppose you mean that you have a dog to help you?' Van Cheele guessed.

The boy rolled slowly over on to his back, and laughed a strange, low laugh. At one and the same time it sounded pleasant, and disagreeable. It had something of the character of a kind of animal noise.

'I don't believe any dog would want to go hunting with me, especially at night.'

Van Cheele began to feel that there was something most unusual about the strange-eyed, strange-talking boy.

'Well, I don't want you staying in these woods. They belong to me,' he declared.

'I expect you would rather have me here than in your house,' said the boy.

The thought of this wild, unclothed person walking about Van Cheele's well-ordered house was certainly a frightening one.

'If you don't go willingly, I shall have to make you go,' said Van Cheele.

The boy turned like a flash, dived into the pool, and in less than a second, had flung his wet, gleaming body half-way up the bank where Van Cheele was standing. In an animal like an otter, the movement would not have been anything unusual; in a boy, Van Cheele thought it quite terrifying. His foot slipped as he stepped backward, and he found himself almost flat on his back, sitting on the slippery grassy bank, with those tigerish yellow eyes not very far from his own. Without thinking, he half raised his hand to his throat, as if to protect it. The boy laughed again, a laugh which sounded more animal-like than ever. With another of his astonishing, lightning movements, he quickly ran off into a patch of small bushes and tall grass.

'What an extraordinary creature!' said Van Cheele as he picked himself up. And then he remembered Cunningham's remark, 'There is a wild animal in your woods.'

Not his usual self

Walking slowly homeward, Van Cheele began to think about various things that had happened in the neighbourhood recently, and which might have been caused by this astonishing young savage.

Something had been killing the wild animals in the woods lately — ducks and chickens had been missing from the farms, hares were hardly ever seen, when they should have been quite common, and he had heard farmers complaining about lambs disappearing from fields up in the hills. Was it possible that this wild boy was really hunting the countryside in company with some clever dog? He had spoken of hunting 'on four feet' by night, but then, again, he had hinted strangely at no dog wanting to come near him, 'especially at night.' It was certainly puzzling.

Then, as Van Cheele thought about the various problems that had occurred during the last month or two, he came suddenly to a complete stop, both in his walking and in his thinking. That child missing from the mill two months ago — people thought that it had fallen into the river and been carried away; but the mother had always said she had heard a loud cry coming from the hillside, and from the opposite direction to the river. It was ridiculous to think such a thing, of course, but he wished that the boy had not made that strange remark about child-meat eaten two months ago. Such dreadful things should not be said, even in fun.

When he got home, Van Cheele did not feel like talking about his discovery in the wood. It seemed to him that his position as a leader of village society might be in danger, if it became known that such a strange, and possibly wicked, person was living somewhere on his property. He might even be asked to pay for the lambs and other animals that had been killed. At dinner that night, he was unusually silent.

'Lost your tongue, have you?' said his aunt. 'One would think you had seen a wolf.'

Van Cheele thought his aunt's remark rather foolish. If he had seen a wolf, his tongue would have been working extraordinarily busily.

At breakfast next morning Van Cheele's uneasiness regarding the strange meeting had not completely disappeared. He decided to go by train to the neighbouring town, find Cunningham, and learn from him what had really caused him to mention a wild animal in the woods.

The poor lost boy

With this decision taken, his cheerfulness returned, and he sang a bright little tune as he wandered into the morning-room for his usual after-breakfast cigarette. As soon as he had entered the room, however, the song stopped.

'Heavens!' he cried out in astonishment.

Gracefully stretched out on the sofa, looking as if he had never before been so comfortable in his life, was the boy from the woods. He was drier than when Van Cheele had last seen him, but no other alteration was noticeable in his appearance.

'How dare you come here?' Van Cheele said furiously.

'You told me I was not to stay in the woods,' said the boy calmly.

'But not to come here. Supposing my aunt should see you!'

Van Cheele hastily covered as much of his unwelcome guest as possible under the sheets of *The Morning Post*. At that moment his aunt walked in.

'This is a poor boy who has lost his way — and lost his memory. He doesn't know who he is or where he is from,' explained Van Cheele. He looked nervously at the boy's face to see whether he was going to make any embarrassing remarks, or movements.

Miss Van Cheele was greatly interested.

'Perhaps his clothing has his name marked on it,' she suggested.

'He seems to have lost that, too,' said Van Cheele, making anxious little grabs at the sheets of *The Morning Post* to keep them in place.

Miss Van Cheele regarded this naked homeless child as warmly as she would have looked upon a lost kitten or an unwanted puppy.

'We must do all that we can for him,' she said.

A nice suitable name

A messenger was sent to a neighbour's house where they kept a boy-servant of about the right size. In a very short time he returned with a servant's uniform: a shirt, shoes, collar, etc. Even when he was clothed, clean and tidy, however, the boy lost none of his strangeness, Van Cheele thought. His aunt found him quite sweet, though.

'We must call him something until we know who he really is,' she said. 'Gabriel-Ernest, I think. That is a nice name, and it suits him very well.'

Van Cheele agreed that Gabriel-Ernest was a nice name, but he privately doubted whether it was being given to a nice boy.

His doubts were not reduced by the fact that his elderly dog had rushed out of the house when the boy arrived. It now stood shivering and barking fearfully at the farther end of the orchard. The caged bird, too, usually as cheerful a singer as Van Cheele himself, gave out no more than a series of frightened little cheeps. More than ever, Van Cheele felt he needed to talk to Cunningham.

As he left the house to drive to the station, his aunt was arranging that Gabriel-Ernest should help her to entertain the ten or twelve small children in her Sunday-school class. They were to come to tea that afternoon.

The Greek god

Cunningham did not, at first, want to talk about what he had seen. 'My mother died of some sort of brain trouble,' he explained, 'so you will understand why I do not wish to discuss anything of an impossibly strange nature that I may have seen, or that I may think I have seen.'

'But what did you see?' persisted Van Cheele.

'What I thought I saw was something so extraordinary that only a mad person would believe it had actually happened. I was standing, the last evening I was with you, half-hidden in the hedge by the orchard gate, watching the last light of the sunset. Suddenly I noticed a naked boy standing out on the hillside, and also watching the sunset. I took him to be a swimmer from some neighbouring pool. He looked so much like one of those wild Greek gods that I immediately wanted to paint a picture of him. In another moment I think I should have called to him, but just then the sun sank from view, and all the soft colours slid out of the sky, leaving everything looking cold and grey. And at the same moment an astonishing thing happened. The boy disappeared, too!'

'What! You mean the boy was there one moment, and gone the next?' asked Van Cheele.

'No, that is the dreadful part of it,' answered the artist. 'On the open hillside where the boy had been standing a second before, I could see a large black wolf, with long, sharp teeth and cruel, yellow eyes. You may think —'

But Van Cheele did not stop to think about anything. Already he was running at top speed towards the station.

The rescue attempt

Van Cheele thought he might send a telegram: 'Gabriel-Ernest is a werewolf,' but then he realized that he would never be able to express, in just a few words, how terribly dangerous the boy was. Also, his aunt knew nothing of werewolves —

creatures that were half wolf, half human being. She would just think the telegram was a secret message, and that Van Cheele had forgotten to give her the key. His one hope was that he might get home before sunset.

The cab that he hired at the other end of the railway journey carried him, with what seemed maddening slowness, along the country roads, through a countryside filled with the colours of the sinking sun. His aunt was putting away the tea things, and some unfinished cake when he arrived.

'Where is Gabriel-Ernest?' he almost screamed.

'He is taking the Toop child home,' said his aunt. 'It was getting so late, I thought it wasn't safe to let the little boy go back alone. What a lovely sunset, isn't it?'

But Van Cheele did not stay to discuss the beauties of the evening sky. He raced along the narrow lane that led to the home of the Toops.

On one side of the road, the river ran dark and swift, on the other was the bare hillside. The red sun showed still on the horizon, and the next turning must bring him in view of the two people he was chasing. But then the colour went suddenly out of things, and a grey light settled itself with a quick shiver over the countryside. Van Cheele heard a cry of fear. He stopped running.

Nothing was ever seen again of the Toop child or Gabriel-Ernest, but Gabriel-Ernest's clothes were found lying in the road. Everyone said that the little boy must have fallen into the water, and that Gabriel-Ernest had taken off his clothes and jumped in after him, in attempt to rescue him. Van Cheele and some workmen, who were nearby at the time, said they had heard a child scream loudly just near the place where the clothes were found.

Miss Van Cheele was greatly saddened by the loss of Gabriel-Ernest. She had a memorial put up in the village church. It said: 'Gabriel-Ernest, an unknown boy, who bravely gave his life trying to save another.'

Van Cheele usually did everything his aunt asked him to do, but he absolutely refused to give any money to the Gabriel-Ernest memorial.

5
ANXIOUS MOMENTS

LOUISE

Unusually clever

'The tea will be quite cold, you'd better ask the servants to bring some more,' said Lady Beanford.

Lady Susan Beanford was a lively old woman who had thought herself quite ill for most of her life. Someone once said that once she had caught a cold, she never let it go again. Her younger sister, Jane Thropplestance, was mainly famous for being the most forgetful woman in London.

'I've really been unusually clever this afternoon,' Jane said, as she sat down in a comfortable armchair by the fire. 'I've visited all the people I planned to visit, and I've done all the shopping that I wanted to do. I even remembered to try and find the silk cloth you wanted at Harrods, but I had forgotten to take the colour sample you gave me, so it was no use. I really think that was the only important thing I forgot during the whole afternoon. Quite wonderful for me, isn't it?'

'But where is Louise?' asked her sister. 'Didn't you take her out with you? You said you were going to.'

'Good God!' exclaimed Jane. 'What have I done with Louise? I must have left her somewhere.'

'But where?'

'That's just it. Where have I left her? I can't remember if the Carrywoods were at home or if I just spoke to the servants and left my name card to say I had called. If they were at home, I may have left Louise with them. I'll go and telephone Lord Carrywood and find out: he will be at home by now, I am sure.'

'Is that you, Lord Carrywood?' she asked over the telephone. 'It's me, Jane Thropplestance. I want to know, have you seen my niece Louise?'

'You left your name card here this afternoon, but I don't think you left a niece. The servants would have told me if you had. Is it a new fashion to leave nieces with people as well as name cards? I hope not; some houses have no room for that sort of thing.'

'She's not at the Carrywoods,' said Jane, returning to her tea. 'Perhaps I left her at the silk counter at Selfridges. I may have told her to wait there a moment, and then forgotten about her when I realized I did not know which colour you wanted. In that case she's still there. She wouldn't move away; Louise never does anything unless someone tells her.'

Only misplaced

'You said you tried to buy the silk at Harrods, not Selfridges,' interrupted Lady Beanford.

'Did I? Perhaps it was Harrods. I really don't remember. It was one of those places where every one is so kind and sweet and so on. One almost hates to take even a piece of cloth away from such pleasant circumstances.'

'I think you could have at least taken Louise away. I don't like the idea of her being there among a lot of strangers. Suppose some bad person was to start having a conversation with her?'

'Impossible. Louise does not know how to hold a conversation. I've never discovered a single subject on which she'd say anything beyond "Do you think so? I dare say you're right." By the way, this bread and butter is cut far too thin; it falls apart long before you can get it to your mouth. One feels so silly, snapping at one's food in mid-air. It's like a fish jumping out of the water to catch a fly.'

'I am rather surprised,' said Lady Beanford, 'that you can sit there enjoying your food so much when you've just lost your favourite niece.'

'You talk as if I'd lost her in the sense that she has died, when I have only misplaced her for the moment. I'm sure to remember soon where I left her. I'm trying to think whether she was with me when I visited Ada Spelvexit.

I rather enjoyed myself there. But no, I am certain I didn't leave Louise with her.'

'If you could remember where you did leave her, it would be more helpful,' said Lady Beanford. 'So far all we know is that she is not at the Carrywoods or with Ada Spelvexit.'

'Well, that means there are two fewer places to look for her,' said Jane hopefully; 'I rather think she was with me when I went to Mornay's. I know I went to Mornay's, because I remember meeting that delightful Malcolm What's-his-name there — you know whom I mean. That's the great advantage of people having unusual first names, you needn't remember what their other name is. He gave me two theatre tickets for a play at Sloane Square. I've probably left the tickets at Mornay's, but still it was very kind of him to give them to me.'

'Do you think you left Louise there?'

'I might telephone and ask. Oh, Robert,' she said, turning to the servant, 'before you clear the tea-things away, please call up Mornay's, in Regent Street. Ask if I left two theatre tickets and one niece in their shop this afternoon.'

'A niece, ma'am?'

'Yes, Miss Louise didn't come home with me, and I'm not sure where I left her.'

'Miss Louise has been upstairs all afternoon, ma'am, reading. I took up tea to Miss Louise at a quarter to five, ma'am.'

'Of course, how silly of me. I remember now, I asked her to read to Emma while I went out. Of course Louise wouldn't stop doing anything till someone told her to. I expect she's still at it. Anyhow, you can ring up Mornay's, Robert, and ask whether I left two theatre tickets there. Except for your silk cloth, Susan, those seem to be the only things I've forgotten this afternoon. Quite wonderful for me.'

THE GUESTS

The Bishop

'The view from our windows is lovely,' said Annabel. 'Those flowering trees and green fields, and the river winding along the valley — they all make a most effective picture. But there's something terribly sleepy about it. Nothing ever happens here. It's rather boring, don't you think?'

'Not at all,' said Matilda, 'I find it very restful. But then, you see, I've lived in countries where things do happen, ever so many at a time, when you're not ready for them to happen all at once.'

'That, of course, makes a difference,' said Annabel.

'I have never forgotten,' said Matilda, 'the time when the Bishop of Bequar paid us an unexpected visit; he was on his way to some church nearby.'

'I thought that in India you were always ready for unexpected guests,' said Annabel.

'I was quite prepared for half a dozen Bishops,' said Matilda. 'But it happened that this one was a distant cousin of mine. His parents had argued bitterly and noisily with my parents about a set of silver plates. They got them and we ought to have had them. Or we got them and they thought they ought to have had them. Now I forget which; anyhow, I know they behaved disgracefully. And here was their son, turning up as a holy man, so to speak, and asking to stay with us for a few days.'

'What did your husband think?'

'My husband was fifty miles up-country. He was talking to some villagers there that thought one of their leading men was a were-tiger.'

'A what?'

'A were-tiger. You've heard of were-wolves, haven't you, a mixture of wolf and human being and devil? Well, in those parts they have were-tigers, or think they have. And I must say that in this case, they may have been right.'

'Anyway, I hope you weren't unkind to the Bishop.'

'Of course he was my guest, so I had to be polite. But he was silly enough to talk about the old quarrel, and to defend the way his side of the family had behaved. Well, even if he was right — which he wasn't — my house was not the place in which to say it. I didn't argue with him. But I did give my senior cook a holiday to go and visit his old mother.

'The junior cook was not very good. He originally came to us as a gardener, but as we never had a garden, he helped watch the goats. He was quite good at that, I remember. When the Bishop heard that I had sent away the senior cook on a special and unnecessary holiday, he knew he was no longer welcome. We hardly spoke to each other after that. If you have ever had a Bishop with whom you were not speaking as a guest in your house, you will understand what it was like.'

The flood

Annabel said that she had never had such an experience.

'Then,' continued Matilda, 'to make matters even more complicated, the Gwadlipichee River flooded, a thing it did every now and then. The following morning the lower part of the house and all the barns and stables were under water. We got the horses loose in time, and a servant swam with them to the nearest hill. All the space in the house was filled up with wet, tired-looking goats and chickens. Of course, I had been through that sort of thing in floods before. But never before had I had a houseful of goats and half-drowned chickens plus a Bishop with whom I was not speaking.'

'It must have been difficult,' said Annabel.

'It got worse. I wasn't going to let just an ordinary flood wash out the memory of that family quarrel. I made it clear to the Bishop that his large bedroom and his small bathroom were his part of the house, and where he should stay. However, that afternoon, when he woke up from his midday sleep, he suddenly came into the room that was normally the sitting room, but was now dining room, storehouse, barn and half a dozen other things as well.

'"I'm afraid there is nowhere for you to sit," I said coldly, "the room is full of goats and chickens."

'"There is a goat in my bedroom," he said with equal coldness.

'"Really," I said, "so there's one more still alive! I thought all the other goats were dead."

'"This particular goat is quite dead," he said. "It is being eaten by a tiger right now. That is why I left the room; some animals don't like being watched while they are eating."'

A frightening situation

'The tiger, of course was easily explained. It had been looking round for goats when the flood came. It then climbed up by the outside staircase leading to the Bishop's bathroom, thoughtfully bringing a goat with it. Probably it found the bathroom too small, and moved its dinner to the bedroom where the Bishop was sleeping.'

'What a frightening situation!' exclaimed Annabel. 'Having a hungry tiger in the house, with a flood all round you!'

'The tiger, by then, was not at all hungry,' said Matilda. 'It was full of goat, and probably wanted only to go to sleep. Still, it was embarrassing to have my only guest-room occupied by a tiger, the house filled up with goats and wet chickens — and a Bishop with whom I was not speaking in my only sitting-room.

'I really don't know how I got through it all. Of course mealtimes only made matters worse. The junior cook had every excuse for sending in watery soup and wet rice. Fortunately, the Gwadlipichee goes down as rapidly as it rises. Just before dawn, the servant who had left with the horses came splashing back with them.

'Then a problem arose from the fact that the Bishop wished to leave sooner than the tiger did. As the latter was comfortably laid out in the midst of the former's things, there was an obvious difficulty in arranging for the Bishop to leave first.

'I pointed out to the Bishop that a tiger, having just finished an entire goat, needed a certain amount of rest. If I had fired guns to frighten the animal away, as the Bishop suggested, it would probably merely have left the bedroom to come into the already overcrowded sitting room. It was rather a relief when they both finally left. Now, perhaps, you can understand why I like the sleepy countryside so much, where things don't happen.'

MRS PACKLETIDE'S TIGER

To shoot a tiger

Mrs Packletide, who lived in India, very much wanted to shoot a tiger. It wasn't because she suddenly needed to kill something. Nor did she feel that India would be safer than when she had first arrived, if she left it with one less wild beast. No. Her reason was the fact that Loona Bimberton had recently been carried eleven miles in an aeroplane, and talked of nothing else. Everyone was impressed with Loona Bimberton. Mrs Packletide knew that only a tiger-skin and a write-up in the newspapers could successfully equal an achievement of that sort.

Mrs Packletide had already planned in her mind the lunch she would give at her house in Curzon Street, with a tiger-skin rug taking up most of the floor and all the conversation. Loona Bimberton would be the guest of honour, of course.

She had also already planned the tiger tooth necklace that she was going to give Loona Bimberton on her next birthday.

In a world that is supposed to be chiefly moved by hunger and by love, Mrs Packletide was an exception. Almost everything that she did was due to her jealousy of Loona Bimberton. So Mrs Packletide offered a thousand rupees for the opportunity of shooting a tiger without too much trouble to herself.

It so happened that a neighbouring village was the favourite hunting ground of a tiger who was too old and too lazy to kill anything but people's pets and chickens. The villagers were greatly excited at the thought of possibly ridding themselves of this nuisance and at the same time earning the thousand rupees. Children were immediately told to stand on guard night and day by the edge of the local jungle. Their job was to chase the tiger back towards the village if he seemed to be leaving for other hunting grounds. With well-planned carelessness, the cheaper kinds of farm animals were left standing about to keep him satisfied where he was.

The one great worry was that he might die of old age before Mrs Packletide arrived to shoot him. Mothers carrying their babies home through the jungle, after the day's work in the fields, stopped their singing for fear of disturbing the restful sleep of the aged tiger.

The kill

The great night finally arrived, moonlit and cloudless. A platform had been built in conveniently-placed tree. There sat Mrs Packletide and her paid companion, Miss Mebbin. A goat was tied up at the correct distance. With a good gun and a tiny pack of playing cards, the sportswoman awaited the coming of the tiger.

'I suppose we are in some danger?' said Miss Mebbin.

She was not actually nervous about the wild beast. She did, however, have a terrible fear of doing even the slightest bit of extra work for which she was not to be paid.

'Nonsense,' said Mrs Packletide, 'it's a very old tiger. It couldn't jump up here even if it wanted to.'

'If it's an old tiger, I think you ought to get it cheaper. A thousand rupees is a lot of money.'

Louisa Mebbin always thought carefully about money, no matter how large or small the amount. But her thoughts on how much money old tiger meat would bring on the market were cut short by the appearance of the animal itself.

As soon as the tiger saw the goat, it lay flat on the earth. It did not do this because that is the way tigers hunt. It did it more for the purpose of taking a short rest before beginning the attack. Then it began walking slowly towards the goat.

'Now, now!' cried Miss Mebbin with some excitement. 'If he doesn't touch the goat, we needn't pay for it.'

The gun flashed out with a loud noise. The great tiger leaped to one side and then rolled over, still and dead. In a moment a crowd of excited natives had run on to the scene, and their shouting speedily carried the glad news to the village. But their joy was nothing compared to that of Mrs Packletide.

Extra expenses

It was Louisa Mebbin who pointed out that the goat was dying from a bullet-wound, while no sign of the gun's deadly work could be found on the tiger. Clearly the wrong animal had been hit, and the old tiger had died of heart-failure, caused by the sudden noise.

Mrs Packletide was naturally annoyed at the discovery. But, at any rate, she had a dead tiger, and the villagers, anxious for their thousand rupees, gladly agreed with the story that she had shot the beast. And Miss Mebbin's wages were paid by Mrs Packletide. Therefore, Mrs Packletide faced the reporters' cameras with a light heart, and her picture soon appeared in magazines all over the world.

Loona Bimberton, meanwhile, refused to look at any magazines for weeks, and her letter of thanks for the gift of a tiger-tooth necklace was as short as could still be considered polite. She turned down the invitation to the luncheon-party, however; there are limits to politeness.

From Curzon Street the tiger-skin rug travelled down to the Packletide's country house, and was looked at and admired by neighbours from near and far. It seemed quite suitable for Mrs Packletide to go to the New Year's Ball dressed as Diana, the Goddess of the Hunt.

A few days after the New Year's Ball, Louisa Mebbin said to Mrs Packletide, 'How amused everyone would be if they knew what really happened.'

'What do you mean?' asked Mrs Packletide quickly.

'How you shot the goat and frightened the tiger to death,' said Miss Mebbin, with a laugh.

'No one would believe it,' said Mrs Packletide, her face changing colour.

'Loona Bimberton would,' answered Miss Mebbin. Mrs Packletide's face became an unpleasant greenish white.

'You surely wouldn't tell anyone?' she asked.

'I've seen a weekend house near Dorking that I want to buy,' said Miss Mebbin. 'Six hundred and eighty pounds. It's not an awful lot of money, really, but I just can't afford it.'

Louisa Mebbin's pretty weekend house near Dorking is the wonder and admiration of her friends. It is called 'Les Fauves', which is French for 'wild animals'. Most people believe it was given that name, because in summer-time the garden is gay with many flowers, including tiger-lilies.

Mrs Packletide has tried no more tiger hunting. 'The extra expenses are too heavy,' she tells her friends.

6

THE REMOULDING OF GROBY LINGTON

Visiting relatives

Groby Lington was waiting in the morning-room of his sister-in-law's house. About a quarter of an hour would have to pass before the time came to say his goodbyes. He would then make his way through the village to the station, in the company of his nephews and nieces.

Like many men in advanced middle age, he felt the need to fill the time while he waited, and he began looking around the room for something to do.

He was a kind, good-natured man. He always said how delighted he was to pay occasional visits to the wife and children of his dead brother William. In practice, however, he much preferred the comfort of his own house and garden, and the companionship of his books and his parrot. The truth was he found the experience of visiting this family of young people both meaningless and rather uninteresting. He went from time to time, but it was not his conscience that forced him to make the occasional short trip by rail to see his relatives. What worried him most was the thought that his older brother, Colonel John, would accuse him of being cold-hearted and of forgetting about poor William's family.

Groby usually ignored the existence of his nearby relatives, until he heard that the Colonel was about to visit him. Then he would make a hurried trip across the few miles of country that lay between him and them in order to see the young people again, and take a rather uneasy interest in the well-being of his sister-in-law. On this occasion he had left the visit so late that he would scarcely reach his home before the Colonel was due to arrive there. Anyhow, he had done his duty, he said to himself. Now, six or seven months could pass before he would need to give up his comforts and his interests in order to meet the younger members of the family again.

This happy thought made him quite cheerful as he hopped about the room, picking up first one object, then another, taking a quick look at each like an old bird pecking at its food.

The picture

Groby's cheerfulness did not last for long, however. It suddenly changed to an attitude of angry attention. In a book of drawings, belonging to one of his nephews, he had come across a cleverly drawn picture of himself and his parrot. They appeared to be facing each other like two elderly gentlemen who had just met in the street. They were drawn to look like one another in a way that the artist had done his best to exaggerate.

After the first feelings of anger had passed, Groby laughed good-naturedly. He told himself that the drawing was a clever one, and there was some truth in it. Then the feeling of anger returned. He was not angry with the artist who had expressed the idea in pen and ink, but against the idea itself. Did people really change so that they looked like the animals they kept as pets? Had he unconsciously become more and more like the parrot, the ridiculous old bird that was his constant companion?

Groby was unusually silent as he walked to the train with his chattering nephews and nieces. During the short railway journey, he became more and more certain that he had gradually grown into a sort of parrot-like existence. Every day his life was calm and careless; he wandered about in his garden, among his fruit trees, or sat in his chair on the lawn, or by the fireside in his library. And what was the sum total of his conversation with any neighbours he might meet? 'Quite a lovely spring day, isn't it?' 'It looks as though we might have some rain, later.' 'Glad to see you about again; you must take care of yourself.' 'How fast the young folk grow up, don't they?' Stupid remarks like this were all that he could remember, remarks that were certainly not the intelligent exchange of human minds, but just a lot of empty parrot-talk. One might really just as well greet one's friends and neighbours with 'Pretty Polly. Puss, puss. Miaow, miaow!' Groby began to hate the picture of himself as a foolish, bird-like old creature, which his nephew's drawing had first suggested, and which his own self-accusing imagination was filling in with such detail.

'I'll give the stupid bird away,' he said, though he knew at the same time that he would do no such thing. It would look so ridiculous if, after all the years that he had kept the parrot and told everyone how much he liked it, he suddenly tried to find it a new home.

A new pet

Groby's own small carriage, driven by his own stable-boy, came to meet him at the station.

'Has my brother arrived?' he asked the lad.

'Yes sir, he came down by the two-fifteen. Your parrot's dead, sir.' The stable-boy announced this tragedy in an important-sounding voice, and quite uncaring about the feelings of his listener.

'My parrot dead?' said Groby. 'What caused its death?'

'The ipe,' said the boy briefly.

'The ipe?' asked Groby. 'Whatever's that?'

'The ipe. The Colonel brought it with him,' came the rather frightening answer.

'Do you mean that my brother is ill?' asked Groby. 'Is the ipe some sort of dangerous disease?'

'The Colonel's very well,' said the lad, and as he had no more information to offer, Groby remained puzzled till he reached home. His brother was waiting for him in the hall.

'Have you heard about the parrot?' he asked at once. 'I'm awfully sorry. As soon as he saw the monkey I'd brought as a surprise for you, he called out, 'Rats to you, sir!' and the monkey jumped straight at him, got him by the neck and started twisting it round and round. The poor bird was as dead as cold meat by the time I'd got him away from the little beast. He has always been such a friendly little animal, that monkey has. I would never have thought he could have got as angry as all that. I can't tell you how sorry I feel about it, and now of course you'll hate the sight of the little ape.'

'Not at all,' said Groby sincerely, realizing that the 'ipe' he had been warned of was not a dangerous disease, but the lad's way of saying the word 'ape'.

A few hours earlier Groby would have seen the death of his parrot as a tragedy. Now, with the unexpected departure of his old friend, it seemed almost as if the gods were being kind to him.

'The parrot was very old, you know,' Groby said, in explanation of his lack of sadness at the loss of his pet. 'I was really beginning to wonder if I should let him go on living. He would have suffered, poor old thing, and it would have been cruel to keep him alive. But what a charming little monkey!' he added, when he was introduced to the murderer of the poor bird.

The newcomer was a small, long-tailed South American monkey. It had a gentle, half-shy, half-trusting look that Groby instantly liked. Someone who knew a lot about monkeys, however, might have seen the occasional red light in its eyes as a sign of the bad temper which the parrot had set going with such surprising results for itself.

The servants had liked old Polly. They thought of the dead bird as a member of the family, and one who never caused them much trouble. They were shocked when they saw that his bloodthirsty killer had been accepted in his place as a well-loved pet.

'A nasty trouble-making little ipe what don't never say nothing sensible and cheerful, same as poor Polly did,' was the judgement coming from those who worked in the kitchen.

Miss Wepley's sweets

One Sunday morning, some twelve or fourteen months after this event, Miss Wepley was sitting in church, immediately in front of Groby Lington. She had not lived in the neighbourhood as long as most of the other churchgoers, and she had never been introduced to Groby, who always sat in the row behind her. However, for the past two years, attendance at the Sunday morning church service had brought each of them regularly within sight and sound of one another. Without being at all friendly, they both knew each other quite well. Miss Wepley knew how Groby Lington spoke when he said his prayers. Groby Lington was well aware of the unimportant fact that Miss Wepley always placed a small paper packet of sweets on the seat beside her. She hardly ever felt the need to use them, but she brought them with her in case she should start coughing.

On this particular Sunday, the sweets were the cause of something far more troubling than an attack of coughing. As she stood up to take part in the singing, she thought she saw the hand of Groby Lington, who was alone in the row of seats behind her, make a quick downward grab at the packet of sweets lying on the seat. She turned to see what was happening. She found that the packet had most certainly disappeared, but the mind of Mr Lington was, it seemed, fixed firmly on his singing.

Miss Wepley glared at Groby Lington. She knew he had taken her sweets. But no matter how angrily she glared, Groby's face looked as innocent as an angel's.

'Worse was to follow,' as she said afterwards to a shocked audience of friends. 'I had only just knelt down for the prayers when a sweet, one of my sweets, went shooting past my face, just under my nose. I turned round and stared hard at him, but Mr Lington had his eyes closed and his lips moving as if he were praying. The moment I turned my head, a second sweet flew past and went rolling along the floor, and then a third. I took no notice for a while, and then turned round suddenly just as the dreadful man was about to throw another one at me. He quickly pretended to be turning over the pages of his prayer-book, but he was too late: I had seen the truth. He knew that he had been discovered and no more sweets came by. Of course when I go to church next time, I shall sit as far away as possible from Mr Groby Lington.'

'No gentleman would have done such a disgraceful thing,' said one of her listeners, 'and yet Mr Lington used to be such a nice man, and so well respected by everybody. He seems to have behaved like a bad-mannered little schoolboy.'

'He behaved like an ape,' said Miss Wepley.

The clothes thief

About this time, judgement of Groby's behaviour similar to Miss Wepley's was heard in other places. Groby Lington had never been a hero in the eyes of his servants, but he had shared the approval they had given to his parrot. They thought of Groby as a cheerful, pleasant old boy, who gave them no particular trouble. Recently, however, he seemed to have changed.

The stable-boy was one of the first to complain, and he had fairly good reason to do so.

On an unusually hot summer afternoon, the lad had received permission to bathe in a pond in the orchard. Shortly afterwards, Groby, hearing loud shouts of anger mixed in with the chattering of monkey-language, went to see what was happening. He found his small, fat stable-boy, dressed only in a jacket and a pair of socks, jumping about, red faced with anger, and shaking his fist at the monkey. The monkey was seated on a long, low branch of an apple tree, carelessly examining a pair of trousers, which he had removed just out of the lad's reach.

'That ipe has taken my clothes,' cried the boy, explaining what was already perfectly clear. The fact that he was only half-dressed made him feel uncomfortable, but at the same time he was pleased to see Groby coming. He believed his master would help him get back his trousers.

An artistic dance

The monkey had stopped its rude chattering. No doubt, with a little help from Groby, it would hand back the stolen property.

'If I lift you up,' suggested Groby, 'you will just be able to reach.'

The boy agreed, and Groby grabbed him firmly by the jacket, which was about all there was to catch hold of, and lifted him off the ground. Then, with surprising strength, Groby twisted round quickly and threw him. The lad went crashing into a patch of tall, green stingingnettles, which closed neatly around him as he fell.

Stinging nettles on bare skin feel like fire, and the lad was not the sort of person who could quietly ignore his own pain and suffering: if he hurt, he yelled. On this occasion the amount of sound that he produced because of his pain, anger and astonishment was great and long-lasting. But above his roars, he could hear the happy chattering of his enemy in the tree, and laughter from Groby.

The boy did a sort of artistic-looking dance, which would have made him famous in any theatre in London, and which indeed received much applause from Groby Lington. When he stopped, he found that the monkey, and Groby, had disappeared. His clothes were lying scattered about on the grass at the foot of the tree.

'They're both ipes, that's what they are,' he said angrily to himself. His judgement might have been a little unkind, but at least it was not without reason.

It was a week or two later that the maid left, having been terrified almost to tears by the master's sudden anger on receiving some under-cooked meat. 'He glared at me and banged his teeth at me, he did really,' she informed the other servants.

'If he did that to me, I'd have something to say to him, I would,' said the cook bravely. But her cooking from then on showed much improvement.

The man who snored

It was not often that Groby Lington joined a house-party. He did not like being away from his own home. He liked it less when he discovered that his hostess, Mrs Glenduff, had given him a room in the more distant wing of her large, old house. Even worse, she had given him a room next to Leonard Spabbink, the world-famous, and rather large, pianist.

'He plays Liszt like an angel,' said the hostess with a smile.

'He may play Liszt like a fish, for all I care,' Groby had thought to himself, after Mrs Glenduff had gone, 'but I bet he snores. He's just the sort of person who would, and he's the right shape for it. The walls of these rooms are very thin, and if I hear him snoring when I'm trying to get to sleep, there'll be trouble.'

He did, and there was.

Groby's patience lasted about two and a quarter minutes. He walked quickly through the corridor into Spabbink's room, and attacked.

As a direct result of Groby's energetic persuasion, the fat musician sat up, not understanding at all what was happening, and looking like a large ice-cream that is just about to melt. Groby pushed him around until he was completely awake. The fat pianist then lost his temper and slapped his ill-mannered visitor on the hand.

In another moment Spabbink was finding it hard to breath and quite unable to call for help. A sheet was wrapped tightly round his head. His arms and legs were pulled out of bed. His fat body was smacked, pinched, kicked, and bumped across the floor, towards the bathroom. The bath was not deep enough for Groby to drown him in it, but that did not stop him from trying.

For a few moments the room was almost in darkness. The candle had been knocked over in an early stage of the struggle. Its light scarcely reached to the spot where splashings, smacks, splutterings, faint cries for help, and a loud chatter of ape-like anger rose from the war that was being fought around the shores of the bath. A few seconds later the scene was brightly lit up by burning curtains.

The hero

When the members of the house-party rushed out on to the lawn, one end of the building was well on fire. Clouds of black smoke were pouring from the windows.

Some moments passed before Groby appeared. He came, not from the house, but from the lower end of the garden. He was carrying the half-drowned pianist in his arms.

His efforts in the bathroom had not achieved the effect he intended. He had then remembered the deeper waters of the garden pond.

The cool night air calmed Groby's anger, and he decided to return the pianist to his room. He then discovered that everyone thought he had rescued poor Leonard Spabbink. They called him a hero. They loudly praised him for his courage. They spoke of the clever way he had tied a wet cloth round the head of the musician to protect him from breathing in the smoke. Groby happily accepted their congratulations. He told everyone in great detail how he had found the musician asleep with an overturned candle by his side and the fire well started.

Spabbink told the story from his point of view some days later, when he had partly recovered from the shock of having

THE REMOULDING OF GROBY LINGTON

been attacked at midnight and half drowned in cold water. But the gentle smiles and whispers with which his tale was greeted warned him that his audience thought his brain had probably been affected by the shock of the fire. He refused, however, to attend the ceremony at which Groby Lington was presented with a life-saving medal by the Royal Humane Society.

It was about this time that Groby's pet monkey fell ill and died. The cold weather and stormy skies of England had not suited it. Its master was greatly saddened by its loss, and never quite recovered his good spirits.

Colonel John brought him a tortoise on his last visit. Now Groby wanders slowly about his lawn and kitchen garden, in company with the tortoise, and showing none of his former cheerful energy. His nephews and nieces have good reason to call him 'Old Uncle Groby'.

TROUBLESOME TIMES

THE BROGUE

The crazy horse

The hunting season was over, but the Mullets had still not been able to sell one of their horses, called the Brogue. The family had hoped for years that someone would buy the Brogue before the hunting was over. But hunting seasons came and went and still the horse was theirs.

The animal had been named 'Crazy One' at first, but it was later renamed 'the Brogue.' Now a 'brogue' is a way of talking that you hear used by people who live in the countryside, and if you talk like that, you will know it is very difficult to stop. If you have a brogue, you can't get rid of it easily. That is exactly what the Mullets felt about their horse. Someone in the neighbourhood had suggested that the first letter of its name was not necessary: the horse was such a wild, wicked creature that 'Rogue' seemed even more suitable.

Toby Mullet had ridden him for four seasons. The Brogue knew the countryside well, having personally made most of the holes in the hedges for many miles around.

The Brogue's manners and general character were not ideal for hunting, but he was probably safer to ride in a hunt than on country roads. According to the Mullet family, he was not really *afraid* of roads, but there were one or two things which caused him to jump about rather wildly. He could ignore motor cars and bicycles. But pigs, small farm-carts, piles of stones by the roadside, push-chairs with babies in, and very white gates, all made him start off suddenly, in a clear imitation of the speed and uncertain direction of a flash of lightning. If a bird flew noisily off the ground, the Brogue would spring into the air at the same moment, but this may have been just to keep it company.

A disaster

It was about the third week in May that Mrs Mullet, mother of Toby and a number of daughters, met Clovis Sangrail in the village. She told him all the local news, speaking with great excitement.

'You know our new neighbour, Mr Penricarde?' she said. 'He is very rich, owns several businesses in Cornwall, middle-aged and rather quiet. Well, he's now living in the Red House, and Toby's sold him the Brogue!'

Clovis spent a moment or two considering this amazing news; then he told her how happy he was to hear of their good fortune. If he was a more emotional type, he probably would have kissed Mrs Mullet.

'How wonderfully lucky to have done it at last! Now you can buy a decent horse. I've always said that Toby was clever. Ever so many congratulations.'

'Don't congratulate me. It's the most unfortunate thing that could have happened!' said Mrs Mullet dramatically.

Clovis stared at her in amazement.

'You see,' said Mrs Mullet, in a low, excited whisper, 'Mr Penricarde rather likes Jessie. I was a fool not to have seen it sooner. Yesterday, at a garden party, he asked her what her favourite flowers were. She told him roses, and today a large bunch of roses arrived, with a box of chocolates that he must have got from London. And he's asked her to play golf with him tomorrow. And now, just at this important moment, Toby has sold him that horse. It's a disaster!'

'But you've been trying to get rid of the horse for years!' said Clovis.

'I've got a houseful of daughters,' said Mrs Mullet, 'and I've been trying — well, not to get rid of them, of course, but a husband or two would certainly be welcome. There are six of them, you know.'

'I don't know,' said Clovis, 'I've never counted. But I expect you're right as to the number. Mothers generally know about these things.'

'And now,' continued Mrs Mullet, in her dramatic whisper, 'when there's a rich man who might actually marry one, Toby sells him that terrible animal. It will probably kill him if he tries to ride it; anyway it will kill any love he might have felt towards Jessie. What is to be done? We cannot very well tell him the truth. You see, we praised the Brogue so highly to him and said it was a wonderful animal.'

'Well, Jessie must try to get it back from Penricarde. She can say it was her favourite. She can say it was sold only because her brother mistakenly thought she was tired of it.'

'It sounds strange to ask for a horse back when you've just sold it,' said Mrs Mullet, 'but something must be done, and done at once. The man is not used to horses, and I believe I told him it was as quiet as a lamb. After all, lambs go kicking and twisting about as if they're mad, don't they?'

'The idea that lambs are calm, gentle little creatures is entirely false,' agreed Clovis.

Jessie is worried

Jessie came back from the golf game the next day both happy and worried.

'It's all right about the marriage,' she said. 'He proposed at the sixth hole. I said I must have time to think it over. I accepted him at the seventh.'

'My dear,' said her mother, 'I think it would have been better to show a little more hesitation, as you've not known him for long. You might have waited until the ninth hole.'

'The seventh is a very long hole,' said Jessie. 'Besides, having to think about the marriage was making us both play very badly. By the time we'd got to the ninth hole we'd settled lots of things. The honeymoon is to be spent in Greece, with perhaps a quick visit to Rome if we feel like it, and a week in London to end up with. Two of his cousins are to be asked to be bridesmaids, so with my sisters there will be seven, which is rather a lucky number. You are to wear your grey silk dress.

'By the way, he's coming over this evening to ask your permission. So far all's well, but about the Brogue it's a different matter. I told him the story about how much we wanted to buy the horse back, but he seems to want to keep it. He said he must have a horse now that he's living in the country, and he's going to start riding tomorrow.

'He's ridden a few times before this on an animal that was used to carrying 80-year-olds and people taking rest cures. That's about all his experience with horses — oh, and he rode a small horse once in Norfolk, when he was fifteen and the small horse twenty-four. And tomorrow he's going to ride the Brogue! I shall be a widow before I'm married, and I do so want to see what Greece is really like; it looks such an interesting place on the map.'

Clovis was sent for immediately, and told the situation.

'Nobody can ride that animal with any safety except Toby,' said Mrs Mullet. 'Only Toby knows exactly what frightens it, and so he is prepared for anything the Brogue decides to do.'

White gates and pigs

'I did hint to Mr Penricarde — to Vincent, I should say — that the Brogue didn't like white gates,' said Jessie.

'White gates!' exclaimed Mrs Mullet. 'Did you mention what effect a pig has on him? Every time he leaves his house, he'll have to go past Lockyer's farm to get to the high road, and there's sure to be a pig or two playing about in the lane.'

'The Brogue doesn't like turkeys either,' said Toby. 'And they have hundreds of them at Lockyer's.'

'It's obvious that Penricarde mustn't be allowed to ride that animal,' said Clovis. 'At least not till Jessie has married him. I tell you what: ask him to a picnic tomorrow, starting at an early hour. He's not the sort to go out for a ride before breakfast. Then, the day after that, I'll find an excuse to take him out on a drive with me. The Brogue will be standing idle in the stable for two days, so Toby can offer to exercise it; then, when he takes it out, it might hurt its foot or something of the sort and conveniently become lame. Penricarde won't be able to ride it for a few more days. If you hurry up with the wedding a bit, the story about the horse hurting its foot can be kept going till the ceremony is safely over.'

Mrs Mullet was an emotional type: she kissed Clovis.

A pleasing sense of humour

It was nobody's fault that it poured with rain the next morning, making a picnic impossible. It was also nobody's fault, but plain ill-luck, that the weather cleared up in the afternoon so that Mr Penricarde could try his first ride with the Brogue.

They did not get as far as the pigs at Lockyer's farm. The church gate was painted a dull green, but it had been white a year or two ago, and the Brogue never forgot he had been in the habit of making a violent turn, twist and jump at this particular point of the road. Then he broke his way into someone's garden, where he found a turkey in a cage. Later, the garden's owner found almost all of the cage lying about here and there, but very little was left of the turkey.

Mr Penricarde was a little shaken and suffered from a hurt knee and some other minor damage. But he good-naturedly blamed his own lack of experience with horses and riding along country roads.

A week or so later there was an article in the local newspaper about the wedding. In the list of wedding presents, the following item appeared: *Brown riding horse, 'The Brogue', bridegroom's gift to the bride.*

'Which shows,' said Toby Mullet, 'that he knew nothing.'

'Or else,' said Clovis, 'that he has a very pleasing sense of humour.'

THE SCHARTZ-METTERKLUME METHOD

The new governess

The train stopped at a small country station. It would not continue on its way for ten minutes, so Lady Carlotta stepped out on to the platform and began to walk up and down its uninteresting length, to kill time. Then, in the road beyond, she saw a cart loaded very heavily, and a horse struggling to pull it along. The driver, from the way he was shouting at the horse and beating it, seemed to hate the animal that helped him earn a living. Lady Carlotta immediately walked over to the cart, and told the driver to be more gentle with the horse.

Some of her friends disapproved of her habit of helping out animals in trouble, saying it was 'none of her business'. Only once had she not interfered. That was when one of these friends was trapped for nearly three hours in a small and extremely uncomfortable tree by a large and angry pig. When that happened, Lady Carlotta, on the other side of the fence, had continued reading her book, and refused to interfere between the pig and its prisoner. It is to be feared that she lost the friendship of the lady in the tree, who finally was rescued by others.

On this occasion, the only thing she lost was her train. She was quite calm about it; her friends and relations were well used to the fact of her luggage arriving without her. She sent a telegram to say that she was coming 'by another train'. Before Lady Carlotta had time to do anything else, however, she was approached by a woman, who seemed to be looking especially carefully at her and her clothes.

'You must be Miss Hope, the new governess,' said the woman.

Lady Carlotta stared at her. 'Very well, if I must I must,' was all she said.

'I am Mrs Quabarl,' continued the woman, 'and where, tell me, is your luggage?'

Losing control

'It's gone off somewhere,' said the so-called 'governess', as if the luggage were in some way to be blamed for its absence. The luggage itself had, in fact, behaved perfectly correctly. 'I've just sent a telegram about it,' she added, which was almost true.

'How annoying,' said Mrs Quabarl. 'These railway companies are so careless. However, my servant can lend you some things for the night,' and she led the way to her car. Lady Carlotta followed. The train had gone and she had nothing to do for a few hours.

During the drive to the Quabarl mansion, Lady Carlotta learned that Claude and Wilfrid were delicate, sensitive young people, Irene was very artistic, and Viola was some other common type of twentieth-century upper-class child.

'I wish them not only to be taught,' said Mrs Quabarl, 'but I want them to be interested in what they learn. In their history lessons, for instance, you must try to make them feel that the stories they learn are about men and women who really lived. Of course, I shall expect you to speak French at mealtimes several days of the week.'

'I shall speak French four days of the week and Russian for the remaining three.'

'Russian? My dear Miss Hope, no one in the house speaks or understands Russian.'

'Oh, I am quite sure I shall not feel terribly embarrassed about that,' said Lady Carlotta.

Mrs Quabarl was beginning to find the new governess surprisingly difficult. She was one of those people who seem, at first, to be very confident, but who lose control of a situation as soon as they are seriously opposed. She expected, for instance, Miss Hope to be impressed by her wealth, and to admire the large, new, expensive car they were riding in. The new governess, however, said she knew that kind of car quite well, and lightly referred to one or two other makes that, she claimed, were much better. Mrs Quabarl felt like an ancient general seeing his heaviest battle-elephant shamefully driven off the field by men with sticks.

At dinner that evening, although helped by her husband, who usually agreed with all her opinions, Mrs Quabarl was unable to regain control. The governess not only helped herself well to wine, but talked with great knowledge about it. The only thing that previous governesses had ever said about wine was that they preferred water. When this one actually recommended a wine seller, Mrs Quabarl thought it time to turn the conversation to more usual subjects.

History

'We got very good references about you from Dr Teep,' said Mrs Quabarl. 'A fine man, and so well respected in his educational work.'

'He drinks like a fish, and beats his wife; otherwise he is a very lovable person,' said the governess calmly.

'My dear Miss Hope! You must be exaggerating,' exclaimed the Quabarls together.

'Of course there is good reason for his behaviour,' continued the naughty Lady Carlotta. 'Mrs Teep is the most annoying card player that I have ever sat down with; the way she plays would make anyone want to hit her. But for Dr Teep to pour the last of the soda-water all over her, on a Sunday evening, when it was impossible to go out and buy any more, shows no thought for the comfort of others. After all, how can you enjoy a drink in the evening without soda-water? You may think me unfair in my judgement, but it was because of that, that I left the Teeps.'

'We will talk of this some other time,' said Mrs Quabarl quickly.

'I shall never speak of it again,' said the new governess with great firmness.

Mr Quabarl changed the subject by asking what studies the new teacher planned to begin with the children the next day.

'History,' she told him.

'Ah, history,' he said. 'Now in teaching them history, you must take care to interest them in what they learn. You must make them feel that they are being introduced to the stories of men and women who really lived —'

'I've told her all that,' interrupted Mrs Quabarl.

'I teach history by the Schartz-Metterklume method,' said the governess.

'Ah, yes,' said her listeners, thinking it wise to pretend they had at least heard the name before.

'What are you children doing out here?' demanded Mrs Quabarl the next morning, on finding Irene sitting at the top of the stairs, looking rather bored, and her sister obviously uncomfortable on the window-seat behind her, with a small carpet almost covering her.

'We are having a history lesson,' came the unexpected reply. 'I am supposed to be Rome, and Viola up there is the she-wolf. Claude and Wilfrid have gone to fetch the poor women.'

'The poor women?'

'Yes, they've got to carry them off. They didn't want to, but Miss Hope said she would punish them if they didn't, so they've gone to do it.'

The baby lion

A loud, angry screaming suddenly was heard outside. The screams were from the two small daughters of the Quabarls' gardener, who were being pulled and pushed towards the house by Claude and Wilfrid. Their job was made even more difficult by the continuous, if not very effective, attacks of the captured girls' small brother. The governess sat carelessly by the front door, watching over the scene like a Goddess of Battles. An angry and repeated cry of 'I'll tell mother!' came from the gardener's children. But their mother, who was deaf, was busy doing some washing, and had no idea of what was happening. Mrs Quabarl flew to the rescue of the struggling girls.

'Wilfrid! Claude! Let those children go at once. Miss Hope, what on earth is the meaning of this scene?'

'Early Roman history; the story of the Sabine women, don't you know? The Romans captured them and made them their wives. It's the Schartz-Metterklume method to make children understand history by acting it out themselves; it fixes it in their memory, you know. Of course, if, thanks to your interference, your boys go through life thinking that the Romans' mothers made them let the Sabine women go, I really cannot be held responsible.'

'You may be very clever and modern, Miss Hope,' said Mrs Quabarl firmly, 'but I should like you to leave by the next train. Your luggage will be sent after you as soon as it arrives.'

'I'm not certain exactly where I shall be for the next few days,' said the governess, 'so please keep my luggage till I wire my address. There are only a couple of boxes and a baby lion.'

'A baby lion!' gasped Mrs Quabarl. Even when she was gone, difficulties created by the new governess would remain behind, it seemed.

'Well, it's actually not a baby any more; it's more than half-grown, you know. A chicken every day and a rabbit on Sundays is what it usually eats. Don't give it raw red meat, though. Raw meat makes it over-excited. Don't worry about getting the car for me, I prefer to walk.'

And Lady Carlotta left the Quabarls' home.

The real Miss Hope had made a mistake as to the day on which she was expected. Her arrival later on the same day that Lady Carlotta left caused a degree of excitement to which Miss Hope was quite unused. The Quabarl family realized they had been fooled, but much relief came with this knowledge.

'How troublesome for you, dear Carlotta,' said her hostess, when Lady Carlotta finally arrived. 'How very annoying, missing your train and having to stop overnight in a strange place.'

'Oh, no,' said Lady Carlotta; 'it was not at all troublesome — not for me.'

8

A QUIET LIFE

THE SILENCE OF LADY ANNE

A general observation

Egbert came into the large, dimly-lit room looking like a man who thinks he might be entering a bomb factory. The little quarrel over the lunch-table had not been fought to a definite finish, and the question was whether Lady Anne wanted to either continue or put a stop to the battle. She now sat stiffly in the armchair by the tea-table; in the darkness of a December afternoon, Egbert could not see the expression on her face.

Don Tarquinio, the cat, lay on the Persian rug, enjoying the firelight, and caring nothing about the moods of Lady Anne.

Egbert poured himself out some tea. As Lady Anne gave no sign of breaking her silence, he made an attempt at opening a conversation. 'My remark at lunch was just a general observation about the way people behave,' he said. 'I was not talking about you, personally.'

Lady Anne remained tight-lipped. The caged bird lazily filled in the silence with a few lines from an Italian song. It was the only song the bird had been taught to sing, and its performance only lasted for a short time.

The silence continued. Usually after four minutes of silence, Lady Anne's anger would become so great that she was forced to speak. This longer silence than usual made Egbert extremely nervous.

To calm himself, he took the milk-jug and poured some milk into Don Tarquinio's dish, but as the dish was already full, an awful overflow was the result. Don Tarquinio looked on with a surprised interest until Egbert asked him to come and drink up some of the spilt milk. At that point the cat looked completely uninterested. Don Tarquinio refused to move. He was prepared to do many things in his life, but he would not allow himself to be used as a carpet-cleaner.

'Don't you think we're being rather foolish?' said Egbert cheerfully.

If Lady Anne thought so, she didn't say.

The promise

'I admit the fault has been partly my own,' continued Egbert, his cheerfulness disappearing quite quickly. 'After all, I'm only human, you know. We all make mistakes. You seem to forget that I'm only human.' He repeated the point, as if someone had suggested that he was not, but in fact Lady Anne had expressed no opinion on the subject either way.

The bird began again its Italian song. Egbert began to feel unhappy. Lady Anne was not drinking her tea. Perhaps she was feeling unwell. But when Lady Anne felt unwell she was not often quiet about it. 'No one knows how I suffer from stomach problems' was one of her favourite statements; but if no one knew, it must have been because they were deaf. The amount of information Lady Anne gave out on the subject of her stomach problems could have filled a book.

Clearly Lady Anne was not feeling unwell.

'I may have been to blame,' Egbert said, taking as much space on the carpet rug as Don Tarquinio would allow him, 'I am willing, if it will help us end this quarrel. I will promise to lead a better life.'

He wondered vaguely how that would be possible. He never did anything his wife could really complain about. But he thought it was the proper thing to say, and was pleased with himself for having said it.

The plan

Lady Anne showed no sign of being impressed.

Egbert looked at her nervously through his glasses.

'I shall go and dress for dinner,' he announced in a voice he intended to sound slightly angry.

A Quiet Life

At the door he stopped and said, 'Aren't we being very silly?'

'The man is a fool,' Don Tarquinio thought to himself as the door closed behind Egbert.

Then he rose from the carpet, stretched, and walked slowly across the room. He leapt lightly on to a bookshelf close to the bird's cage. It seemed to be the first time he had noticed the bird at all, but he was carrying out a plan of action he had worked out earlier that afternoon.

The bird had always thought himself something of a special favourite in that family, and completely safe. Now he pressed himself into a third of his normal size. As Don Tarquinio drew closer, he began helplessly beating his wings and calling out in panic.

The bird was a valuable one. It's unexpected departure from this life would have brought sorrow to both Lady Anne and her husband. But Lady Anne said nothing to the cat. She showed no sign of interfering. For the past two hours, she had been dead.

The Peace of the Farm

A country scene

Crefton Lockyer sat comfortably in the little patch of ground, half-orchard and half-garden, next to a peaceful farmyard. Not only was he comfortable in a physical sense, he was comfortable in his mind, too. After many long years of city life, full of noise and trouble, the peace of his holiday cottage, surrounded by green hills, pleased him more than he had ever expected. If anywhere in the world was like Heaven, this must be it, he thought to himself.

Time and space here seemed to lose all meaning. The minutes slid away into hours. The fields and woodlands fell gradually away into the distance, softly and naturally. Wild weeds from the hedges were growing in the flower-garden, and garden flowers and bushes were, themselves, growing outside their proper place, in the farmyard and the quiet road that went past the farmhouse. Sleepy-looking hens and ducks were equally happy, wandering about the farmyard, orchard, or into the road. Nothing seemed to belong definitely anywhere.

Over the whole scene hung a sense of a peace that was almost magical. In the afternoon you felt that it had always been afternoon, and must always remain afternoon; in the evening you knew that it could never have been anything else but evening.

Crefton Lockyer sat at his ease in the old wooden seat beneath an even older apple tree, and decided that this was the place that his mind had so often dreamed about and that, in recent years, his tired, nervous body had longed to find. He would make this his permanent home. He would live the rest of his life among these simple, friendly country people.

An old witch

As he sat there, working out his plans for the future, an elderly woman came walking slowly through the orchard.

He recognized her. She was a member of the family that lived on the farm, the mother, or possibly the mother-in-law, of Mrs Spurfield, the owner of his holiday cottage. He quickly tried to think of something polite to say, but she spoke to him first.

'There's a bit of writing up on the door over there. What does it say?'

She spoke in a rather bored, tired way, as if the question had been on her mind for years and she hoped, at last, to have it answered. Her eyes, however, looked impatiently over Crefton's head at the door of a small barn, the last of an untidy row of stables, storehouses, and other farm buildings.

Crefton turned to stare at the barn door. He had not noticed any writing there before. 'Martha Pillamon is an old witch' were the words that met his inquiring gaze. He thought carefully before reading them out. Perhaps, he wondered to himself, the person to whom he was speaking was Martha Pillamon herself. It was possible that Mrs Spurfield's name had been Pillamon before she married. And the thin, hard-faced old woman at his side certainly looked like a witch.

'It says something about a person called Martha Pillamon,' he explained.

'What does it say?'

'It's not very polite,' said Crefton. 'It says she's a witch. Such things ought not to be written up.'

'It's true, every word of it,' said his listener with a pleased look on her old face, adding as a special note of her own, 'and she's an ugly old frog, too.'

And as she walked slowly away, she cried out in a thin, high voice, 'Martha Pillamon is an old witch!'

Martha Pillamon

'Did you hear what she said?' whispered a weak but angry voice somewhere behind Crefton's shoulder. Turning round quickly, he saw another old woman — thin, yellow and wrinkled — who seemed to be greatly displeased about what had just been said. Obviously this was Martha Pillamon. The orchard seemed to be a favourite place for the elderly women of the area to walk through, thought Crefton.

'It's lies, it's all wicked lies,' the weak voice went on. 'Betsy Croot is the witch — she and her daughter, the dirty rats. I'll put a spell on them, the old nuisances.'

As she limped slowly away, her eye caught the chalk writing on the barn door.

'What does that say up there?' she demanded, turning round towards Crefton.

'Vote for Soarker,' he replied, with the confidence of someone who had stopped many quarrels.

The old woman grunted, and her discontented muttering gradually grew fainter as she walked lamely away through the trees.

Tea-time

Soon afterwards, Crefton made his way back towards the farmhouse. Somehow much of the peace he had been enjoying seemed to have slipped out of the atmosphere.

Tea-time in the old farm kitchen was usually a very cheerful occasion, and Crefton had found both the food and the company very enjoyable on previous afternoons. Today, however, something seemed to be wrong. There was a kind of sad quietness in the air. No one had much to say to anyone else, and the tea itself, when Crefton came to drink it, was an uninteresting warm, brown soup that would have driven the fun out of the happiest party.

'It's no use complaining about the tea,' said Mrs Spurfield quickly, as her guest stared at his cup as if uncertain what was wrong. 'The kettle won't boil, that's what the trouble is.'

Crefton looked to the kitchen fire. This afternoon it was unusually fierce. On top was a big black kettle. From time to time it sent out a very small puff of steam, but never anything more than that. It seemed to be ignoring the action of the roaring flames beneath it.

'It's been like that for more than an hour, and it just won't boil —' said Mrs Spurfield, adding, by way of complete explanation, 'some old witch has been making trouble for us.'

'It's Martha Pillamon. She's the one who has done it,' said the old mother. 'But I'll give the old frog something to think about. I'll put a spell on her.'

'But it must boil soon,' said Crefton, ignoring their suggestions about the power of black magic. 'Perhaps the wood is damp.'

'It won't boil in time for supper, nor in time for breakfast tomorrow morning, not if you kept the fire burning bright all night long for it,' said Mrs Spurfield. And it didn't.

From then on they lived on fried and baked food. A kind neighbour made tea and sent it across, though it was never hot by the time it reached them.

'I suppose you'll be leaving us now that things have become uncomfortable,' Mrs Spurfield said at breakfast. 'Some people leave as soon as trouble arrives.'

An evil power

Crefton hurriedly said he had no thoughts about changing plans; he noticed, however, that the earlier happiness of the family had mostly gone. Instead they went about looking worried. They were silent most of the time. When they spoke, they made sharp, angry speeches to one another. The old mother sat in the kitchen or the garden all day long, muttering evil spells against Martha Pillamon.

There was something terrifying about the way these weak old women spent most of their time and energy trying to make each other miserable. Hatred seemed to be the one thing they had which was still strong in them. And the strange thing was that some horrible evil power seemed to grow from their hatred and their curses.

No amount of scientific experiment could explain the fact that neither kettle nor cooking pot would bring water to boiling-point even over the hottest fire. Crefton held on as long as possible to the idea that there was something wrong with the coal. But a wood fire gave the same result.

He even bought a small oil-burner, which people use on picnics, and tried that. In and around the farm, when a small kettle was placed on the burner, the water never became more than warm. Further away, it would boil perfectly. After that, Crefton, too, felt that he had come into contact with some unknown and very evil sort of magical force.

Miles away, down through an opening in the hills, he could see a road where motor cars sometimes passed. Yet here, not so very far removed from the modern world, was a peaceful old farm, where something like witchcraft seemed to be powerfully present.

At the duck pond

One morning Crefton walked out through the farm garden on his way to the woods and fields beyond. He wanted to rediscover the comfortable sense of peace that was now so lacking around the farm. Walking through the orchard, he came across the old mother, sitting muttering to herself in the seat beneath the apple tree. 'Let them sink as they swim, let them sink as they swim,' she was repeating over and over again, as a child repeats a half-learned lesson. And now and then she would break off into a cruel laugh, that was not pleasant to hear.

Crefton was glad when he was too far away to hear her any longer. He began to enjoy the quiet loneliness of the shady lanes that seemed to lead nowhere. One, narrower than the rest, attracted him and he decided to walk down it. He was almost annoyed when he found that it really did lead to a small house.

The place looked very quiet and lonely. There was a small vegetable garden — not well looked after — and a few old apple trees standing at the edge of a swift-flowing stream. Closer to him, the water widened into a medium-sized pond before hurrying away again through the dark woodland.

Crefton leaned against a tree trunk and looked across the pond at the poor-looking little home and garden. The only sign of life came from a small line of ducks. At that moment they were marching one after the other down to the water's edge.

There is always something rather interesting in the way a duck changes from a slow, clumsy walker, on land, into a strong, graceful swimmer in the water, and Crefton waited to watch the leader of the line push itself out onto the surface of the pond.

A pitiful sight

He noticed, at the same time, an odd feeling inside himself: something that suggested strange and unpleasant things were about to happen. The duck jumped confidently forward into the water, and dropped immediately under the surface. Its head appeared for a moment and went under again, leaving a train of bubbles, while wings and legs stirred the water as it turned helplessly about, flapping and kicking in terrified panic.

The bird was obviously drowning. Crefton thought at first that it had caught itself in some plants growing in the pond, or it was being attacked by a large fish or water-rat. But no blood floated to the surface, and the wildly struggling body was being carried along by the water without anything holding it back.

A second duck had by this time jumped into the pond, and a second struggling body rolled and twisted under the surface. There was something pitiful in the sight of the terrified heads that showed now and again above the water, clearly completely unable to understand what was happening to them.

Crefton gazed with something like horror as a third duck came to the edge and splashed in. The same thing happened to it, as had happened to the other two. He felt almost relieved when the others, frightened by the noise of their slowly drowning friends, stopped and turned away from the scene of danger, quacking loudly as they went.

The impossible

Crefton became aware that he was not the only human watching this terrible scene. A thin, bent old woman, whom he recognized at once as Martha Pillamon, had limped down the cottage path to the water's edge. She was gazing, horrified, at the dreadful twisting and turning of the dying birds that were being carried in a circle round the middle of the pool. Presently her voice rang out in a scream of anger:

'Betsy Croot has done this, the old rat. I'll put a spell on her — she'll be sorry she ever tried this, she will.'

Crefton walked quietly away, uncertain whether or not the old woman had noticed him. Even before she had declared the guilt of Betsy Croot, however, he had remembered, with horror, how Betsy had been muttering, 'Let them sink as they swim' in the orchard. But it was Martha's threat of revenge, of a spell against old Betsy, that frightened him most. It filled his mind to such an extent that he could no longer think of anything else. He could not afford to ignore the threats these old women made against one another any longer. Clearly it was not just childish nonsense.

Family life at the farm now lay at the mercy of a hard-hearted old woman, who seemed able to express her hatred in a very practical way. Who could tell what form her revenge for three drowned ducks might take? As a visitor living with the family, Crefton, too, might find himself suffering the highly disagreeable effect of Martha Pillamon's anger. Of course he knew that he was being ridiculously silly, but the behaviour of the kettle on the oil-burner, and the scene at the pond had badly frightened him. And the fact that he could not explain his terrors made them seem far worse. Once you start believing that the impossible can happen, the awful possibilities are endless!

Back to city life

Crefton got up early the next morning. He had not slept well: it had been one of the least restful nights he had spent at the farm. He felt quite nervous, and quickly noticed small signs that things were not the way they should be. Clearly this family was in trouble.

The cows had been milked, but they were still standing about in the farmyard, waiting impatiently to be taken to the fields. The chickens were complaining loudly that their food seem to be a long time coming. The noise of the farmyard pump, from which the family frequently drew water during the early morning, was today strangely quiet.

Inside the house itself, footsteps could be heard coming and going; there was a rushing about and dying away of hurried voices, and long, uneasy silences. Crefton finished dressing and walked quietly from his bedroom to the top of a narrow staircase. He could hear a dull, complaining voice, a voice which sounded sad, and quietly defeated. He recognized the speaker as Mrs Spurfield.

'He'll go away, I am sure he will,' she was saying. 'There are those who run away as soon as real misfortune shows itself.'

Crefton felt that he probably was one of 'those', and that there are times when it is best to be true to one's own nature.

He crept back to his room, collected and packed the few things he had brought with him, placed the money due for his stay on a table, and made his way out by a back door into the farmyard. A crowd of noisy hens rushed hopefully towards him. Quickly passing through them, he hurried along until he reached the lane at the back of the farm. A few minutes' walk, which only the weight of his suitcase stopped from turning into a run, brought him to the main road. There he was able to stop a cart driver who offered, for a small price, to speed him on to the neighbouring town. At a bend of the road, he caught a last glimpse of the farm; the old barn, the orchard, and the apple tree, with its wooden seat, could be clearly seen in the early morning light. Over everything hung that mysterious air of magic and witchcraft, which Crefton had once mistaken for peace.

The busy rush and roar of Paddington Railway Station greeted his ears with a noisy, hearty welcome.

'Very bad for our nerves, all this hurrying about,' said a fellow-traveller. 'I prefer the peace and quiet of the country any day.'

In his mind, Crefton threw away his share of the country life — the escape from noise and hurry that so many townspeople dream about. A crowded, brightly-lit music-hall, where a popular song was being played by a group of highly energetic musicians, came nearest to his idea of a rest-cure.

The Way to the Dairy

Caring for an old aunt

The Baroness and Clovis sat in a corner of the park talking about the people who were walking by.

'Who are those sad-looking young women who have just gone past?' asked the Baroness. 'They have the look of people to whom Fate has been especially unkind.'

'Those,' said Clovis, 'are the Brimley Bomefields. I expect you would look sad if you had had their experiences.'

'I'm always having experiences that make me sad,' said the Baroness, 'but I never let anyone know about them. It's as bad as showing people how old you really are. Tell me about the Brimley Bomefields.'

'Well,' said Clovis, 'the beginning of their tragedy was that they found an aunt. The aunt had been there all the time, but they had very nearly forgotten about her until a distant relative reminded them by leaving her something in his will. It is wonderful how quickly people learn from a good example. The aunt, who until then had been poor, became quite pleasantly rich, and suddenly the Brimley Bomefields began to worry about the loneliness of her life. They decided that they should take special care of her. She had a great many people caring for her at that time, many of whom had hardly spoken to her before.'

'Thus far I don't see any tragedy where the Brimley Bomefields are concerned,' said the Baroness.

'We haven't got to that part of the story yet,' said Clovis. 'The aunt had been used to living very simply. She had never had enough money to go away on holiday or give large dinner parties, or generally enjoy herself very much, and her nieces didn't encourage her to waste her newly-acquired wealth. Much of it, they decided, would come to them at her death, and she was a fairly old woman.

'There was one thing, however, which threw a shadow over the pleasure they felt in discovering this attractive old aunt: she openly declared that a large share of her little fortune would go to a nephew on the other side of her family.

'The old aunt's heir was a rather stupid, silly young man, though quite hopelessly clever at thinking up ways of spending money. But he had been kind to the old lady in the days when no one else thought about her, and she took no notice of anything anyone said against him.

'This did not stop her nieces giving her their opinions on that subject. It seemed such a pity, they said, that good money should be given away to such a worthless person. They usually spoke of their aunt's money as "good". That made its presentation to a "bad" young man like the nephew seem doubly unfair.'

Broadening the mind

'Regularly after the Derby, St Leger, and other popular horse-racing events, the Brimley Bomefields talked loudly about how much money they believed Roger had wasted in bets.

'"His travelling expenses must be high," said the eldest Brimley Bomefield one day. "They say he goes to every race-meeting in England, and some in France, too. It wouldn't surprise me if he went all the way to India to attend the Calcutta Sweepstake."

'"Travel, my dear Christine," said her aunt, "gives one a better understanding of the world: it broadens the mind."

'"Yes, dear aunt, if you travel for a good purpose," agreed Christine, "but travel merely for gambling and extravagant living is more likely to reduce the purse than broaden the mind. However, as long as Roger enjoys himself, I suppose he doesn't care how fast or foolishly the money goes, or where he will be able to find more. It seems a pity, that's all."

'The aunt by that time had begun to talk of something else, and it was doubtful if Christine's opinions had even been heard. It was her remark, however — the aunt's remark, I mean — about travel broadening the mind, that gave the youngest Brimley Bomefield her great idea for solving the problem of Roger.

'"If aunt could only be taken somewhere to see him gambling and throwing away his money," she said, "she would understand immediately what a bad character he is. That would be much more effective than anything we could say."

'"My dear Veronique," said her sisters, "we can't go following him about the country to horse-races."

'"Certainly not to horse-races," said Veronique, "but we might go to some place where one can watch the gambling without taking part in it."

'"Do you mean the gambling casinos at Monte Carlo?" they asked her.

'"Monte Carlo is a long way off, and has a bad reputation," said Veronique. "I shouldn't like to tell our friends that we were going to Monte Carlo. But I believe Roger usually goes to Dieppe about this time of year. I know some quite respectable English people who go there, and the journey wouldn't be expensive. If aunt doesn't mind the journey, a little holiday in France might do her a lot of good."

'And that was how the fateful idea came to the Brimley Bomefields.'

Little horses

'Disaster hung over the holiday from the very start, as they afterwards remembered. To begin with, all the Brimley Bomefields were extremely unwell during the sea-crossing, while the aunt enjoyed the fresh air and made friends with all kinds of strange travelling companions. Although it was many years since she had been in France — she had worked there, when she was younger, as a paid companion — her knowledge of the language was very much better than theirs. They found it more and more difficult to take care of a person who knew what she wanted and was able to ask for it, and to see that she got it. Also, as far as Roger was concerned, they were unlucky; it happened that he was staying at Pourville, a little town a mile or two further west. The Brimley Bomefields quickly discovered that Dieppe was too crowded and too silly a place to stay in. They persuaded the old lady to move to the quieter, more respectable atmosphere of Pourville.

'"You won't find it dull, you know," they assured her, "there is a little casino right next to the hotel. You can watch the people dancing and you can watch them throwing away their money at *petits chevaux*." At the time, *petits chevaux* — little horses — was one of the most popular gambling games.

'Roger was not staying in the same hotel, but they knew that he was sure to be present in the casino on most afternoons and evenings.

'On the first evening of their visit, they wandered into the casino after a fairly early dinner, and stood near the game tables. Bertie Van Tahn happened to be staying there, and he described the whole thing to me. The Brimley Bomefields kept a close watch on the doors as though they were expecting someone to arrive, and the aunt got more and more amused and interested watching the little horses race round and round the board.

'"Do you know, poor little number eight hasn't won for the last thirty-two times," she said to Christine. "I've been keeping count. I shall really have to put five francs on him to encourage him."'

The gamblers

'"Do come and watch the dancing, dear," said Christine nervously. It was not part of their plan that Roger should come in and find the old lady placing bets at the *petits chevaux* table.

'"Just wait while I put five francs on number eight," said the aunt, and in another moment, her money was lying on the table.

'The horses began to move round. It was a slow race this time, but number eight crept up at the finish and placed his nose just a fraction in front of number three, who, until then, had seemed to be winning easily. It was so close that the result had to be checked, but number eight was declared the winner. The aunt received thirty-five francs.

'After that, the Brimley Bomefields were quite unable to get the old lady away from the tables. When Roger arrived, she was fifty-two francs richer; her nieces were standing sadly about, not knowing what to do. They looked like chickens that have been hatched out by a duck and, horrified, are watching their mother swimming around in the water, enjoying herself in what seems to them an extremely dangerous element.

The supper-party, which Roger insisted on giving that night in honour of his aunt and the three Miss Brimley Bomefields, was remarkable for the joyful happiness of two of the people there; the remaining guests looked as if they were attending a funeral.

'"I do not think," Christine said afterwards to a friend, who told Bertie Van Tahn, "that I shall ever be able to eat French food again. It would bring back memories of that awful evening."

'For the next two or three days, the nieces made plans for returning to England or moving on to some other holiday town where there was no casino. The aunt was busy working on a system for winning at *petits chevaux*. Number eight, her first love, had not been running so well, and a series of bets on number five had turned out even worse.

'"Do you know, I lost over seven hundred francs at the tables this afternoon," she announced cheerfully at dinner on the fourth evening of their visit.

'"Aunt! That's twenty-eight pounds! And you were losing last night, too."

'"Oh, I shall get it all back," she said, "but not here. These silly little horses are no good. I shall go somewhere where one can play roulette. That is a much better game. You needn't look so shocked. I've always felt that I could be an excellent gambler, and now that you dear things have brought me here, I have the opportunity to try. I must drink to your very good healths. Waiter, a bottle of *Pont et Canet*. Ah, it's number seven on the wine list — I shall put my money on number seven tonight. It won four times running this afternoon when I was betting on that silly number five."'

The good life

'Number seven was not in a winning mood that evening. The Brimley Bomefields, tired of watching disaster from a distance, drew near to the table where their aunt was now a well-known and much respected player, and gazed sadly as one and five and eight and four all won their races, and swept "good money" out of the purse of the loyal follower of number seven. The day's losses came to something very near two thousand francs.

'"What gamblers you are!" said Roger to them, when he found them at the tables.

'"We are not gambling," said Christine, "we are just watching."

'"I don't think so," said Roger, who knew a gambler when he saw one. "Of course you're all in it together, and aunt is putting the bets on for you. Anyone can tell by your looks, when the wrong horse comes in first, that you are very interested in which horse wins, and which loses."

'Aunt and nephew had supper alone that night, or at least they would have if Bertie hadn't joined them; all the Brimley Bomefields had headaches.

'The aunt took them all to Dieppe the next day and set cheerfully about the task of winning back some of her losses. Her luck was variable; in fact, there were a few moments when she had quite good fortune, just enough to keep her amused and interested. But on the whole she lost more than she won. The Brimley Bomefields all had a bad attack of nerves on the day when she sold some of her shares. "Nothing will ever bring that money back," they remarked to one another.

'Veronique, at last, could bear it no longer, and went home. You see, it had been her idea to bring the aunt on this disastrous holiday. Though the others never spoke to her directly about it, there was a certain look in their eyes, which was harder to bear than their words might have been. The other two remained behind. They sadly watched over their aunt until the holiday season in Dieppe came to an end, when they hoped at last to be able to turn her in the direction of home and safety.

'They made anxious calculations as to how little "good money" might, with reasonable luck, be thrown away in the meantime. Here, however, their calculations went completely wrong; the close of the Dieppe season merely turned their aunt's thoughts in search of some other place where she could gamble.

'"Show a cat the way to the dairy —" I forget how the saying ends, but the first part described the situation as far as the Brimley Bomefields' aunt was concerned. She had been introduced to pleasures she had never experienced before, and found them greatly to her liking. She was in no hurry to give up the fruits of her newly-acquired knowledge.

'You see, for the first time in her life, the old thing was thoroughly enjoying herself. She was losing money, but she had plenty of fun and excitement while she was doing it, and she had enough left to live very comfortably on. Indeed, she was only just learning to understand the art of living well. She became a very popular hostess, and in return, her fellow-gamblers were always ready to entertain her to dinners and suppers when their luck was good.'

Retreat

'Her nieces were like sailors on a sinking treasure ship. They were unwilling to leave, thinking it might yet be brought safely into port. But they found little pleasure in their aunt's new way of life. The sight of "good money" being wasted on good living for the entertainment of all sorts of people, none of whom were not likely to be in any way socially useful to them, did not encourage them to take part in the dinners. Whenever possible, they excused themselves from attending; the Brimley Bomefields became famous for their headaches.

'And one day, the nieces realized that, as they would have expressed it, "no useful purpose would be served" by their staying with a relative who had so completely freed herself from their care. The aunt received the news of their departure with a cheerfulness that was almost annoying.

'"It's time you went home and had those headaches seen to by a specialist," was her comment on the situation.

'The homeward journey of the Brimley Bomefields was like Napoleon's retreat from Moscow, and what made it the more bitter was the fact that Moscow, in this case, was not left in flames, but bright with party lights.

'Sometimes friends bring them news of their aunt, who has settled down into being a gambler. Very little remains of the fortune that they hoped would one day be theirs.

'So you need not be surprised,' said Clovis, bringing his story to an end, 'if they do have a rather unhappy look on their faces.'

'Which is Veronique?' asked the Baroness.

'The saddest-looking of the three,' replied Clovis.

10
LIFE'S LITTLE PROBLEMS

TEA

Family hopes

James Cushat-Prinkly was a young man who always knew that he would marry one day, but up to the age of thirty-four he had done nothing at all about it. He liked and admired a great many women generally without picking out one for a wife, just as you might admire the Alps without feeling that you wanted any particular mountain as your own private property.

His unwillingness to come to a decision made his women relatives rather impatient. Whenever he brought a lady friend home, his mother, his sisters, an aunt, and two or three others watched him in the way in which a group of dogs will watch the slightest movements of a human being whom they think might take them for a walk. No decent person can refuse dogs with that sort of look in their eyes, and James Cushat-Prinkly knew how much his family hoped he would find a wife. When his Uncle Jules died and left him a large amount of money, it really seemed he had no excuse but to find someone to share it with him.

Meanwhile, most of his female relatives had already decided on Joan Sebastable. She seemed to be the most suitable young woman among his friends to whom he might propose marriage. James became gradually used to the idea that he and Joan would go together through the usual stages of engagement, congratulations, gift-receiving, the wedding, a holiday in Europe, and after all that, life together in their own home. It was necessary, however, to ask the young lady what she thought about the matter; the family had so far helped the relationship along as much as possible, but the actual proposal would have to be James's own effort.

Tea-time

Cushat-Prinkly walked slowly across the park towards the Sebastable home. He was glad to feel that he was going to get everything settled that afternoon. Proposing marriage, even to a nice girl like Joan, was a troublesome business, but one could not have a honeymoon and then a life of married happiness without proposing first.

His thoughts were interrupted by the sound of a clock striking the half-hour. Half-past four. A frown settled on his face. He would arrive at the Sebastable home just at the hour of their afternoon tea. Joan would be seated at a low table, surrounded by all sorts of silver pots, milk jugs and delicate teacups. She would ask, in a sweet, pleasant voice, a series of little friendly questions about weak or strong tea, how much, if any, sugar, milk, cream, and so forth. 'Is it one lump of sugar or two? I have forgotten: you do take milk, don't you? Would you like some more hot water, if it's too strong?'

Cushat-Prinkly had read of such things, and hundreds of actual experiences had told him that they were true to life. Thousands of women, at this afternoon hour, were sitting behind delicate tea sets, all asking the same little questions.

Cushat-Prinkly hated afternoon tea. According to his own theory of life, a woman should lie on a sofa and talk with charm and wit, or merely sit silently as a thing to be looked upon. From behind a silk curtain, a small servant boy would silently bring in a tray with cups and sweets, place it on a table, and leave it there to be enjoyed. There was no need for all this endless, silly talk about cream and sugar and hot water. If one was really in love, how could one talk sensibly about weak tea!

Cushat-Prinkly had never mentioned this to his mother. All her life she had asked him the same little questions at tea-time from behind her teacups and her silver. If he had spoken to her about sofas and servant boys, she would have thought him crazy.

Now, as he passed through the streets that led to Joan's house, he became horrified at the idea of finding Joan

Sebastable at her tea-table. A way of escape presented itself: on one floor of a narrow little house at the noisier end of Esquimault Street lived Rhoda Ellam. Rhoda was a distant cousin, who made a living by creating hats out of expensive material. The hats really looked as if they had come from Paris. The money she got for them, unfortunately, never looked as if it was enough to take her to Paris. But Rhoda found life amusing and had a fairly good time in spite of her difficult circumstances.

Red pepper and sliced lemon

Cushat-Prinkly decided to walk up to Rhoda's place. The important business which lay before him could wait for half an hour or so. With luck he could thus reach the Sebastable mansion after the last teacups had been cleared away.

Rhoda welcomed him into a room that was her workshop, sitting-room, and kitchen all combined, and which was wonderfully clean and comfortable at the same time.

'I'm having a picnic meal,' she announced. 'There's caviar in that jar by your arm. Begin on that brown bread-and-butter while I cut some more. Find yourself a cup; the teapot is behind you. Now tell me about hundreds of things.'

She said no more about food, but talked amusingly and made her visitor talk amusingly, too. At the same time she cut the bread-and-butter with great skill and brought out red pepper and sliced lemon, where so many women would merely have produced reasons and regrets for not having any.

Cushat-Prinkly found that he was enjoying an excellent tea without having to answer any questions about it at all.

'And now tell me why you have come to see me,' said Rhoda suddenly. 'I hope you've come about hats. I heard that you now have some money, and, of course, I thought that it would be a beautiful thing for you to buy expensive hats for all your sisters. Of course they have not said anything to me about it, but I feel sure they think this way, too.'

'I didn't come about hats,' said her visitor. 'In fact, I don't think I really came about anything. I was passing and I just thought I'd look in and see you. Since I've been sitting talking to you, however, a rather important idea has come to me. Let me tell you what it is.'

Important news

Some forty minutes later, James Cushat-Prinkly returned to his family, with an important piece of news.

'I'm engaged to be married,' he announced.

They were very excited.

'Ah, we knew! We saw it coming! We could tell weeks ago!'

'I'll bet you didn't,' said Cushat-Prinkly. 'If anyone had told me at lunch-time today that I was going to ask Rhoda Ellam to marry me and that she was going to accept, I would have laughed at the idea.'

It was rather difficult for James's women relatives to have to switch their hopes in an instant from Joan Sebastable to Rhoda Ellam but, after all, it was James's happiness that was in question, and his opinion had to be considered.

On a September afternoon of the same year, after the honeymoon abroad had ended, Cushat-Prinkly came into the living-room of his new house in Granchester Square. It was tea-time. Rhoda was seated at a low table, behind a lot of teacups and shining silver. There was a pleasant, sweet note in her voice as she handed him a cup.

'You like it weaker than that, don't you? Shall I put some more hot water in it? No?'

The Story-teller

On the train

It was a fine, summer afternoon, but the train was hot and uncomfortable. The next stop, at Templecombe, was nearly an hour ahead. In the carriage were a small girl, and a smaller girl, and a small boy. The children's aunt sat in one corner seat, and in the corner seat on the opposite side sat a man they did not know. The aunt and the children talked in a dull, persistent way. Most of the aunt's remarks seemed to begin with 'Don't,' and nearly all of the children's remarks began with 'Why?' The man was frowning. He looked quite angry, but said nothing out loud.

'Don't Cyril, don't,' cried the aunt, as the small boy began hitting the cushions of the seat. At each blow a cloud of dust was produced.

'Come and look out of the window,' she added.

The child moved unwillingly to the window. 'Why are those sheep being chased out of that field?' he asked.

'I think they are being taken to another field where there is more grass,' said the aunt weakly.

'But there's lots of grass in that field,' protested the boy. 'There's nothing but grass there. Aunt, there's lots of grass in that field.'

'Perhaps the grass in the other field is better,' suggested the aunt stupidly.

'Why is it better?' was the next question.

'Oh, look at those cows!' exclaimed the aunt. Nearly every field they had passed had contained cows. But now she spoke as though it were something new and amazing.

'Why is the grass in the other field better?' Cyril refused to be tricked into forgetting his question.

The frown on the man's face was growing worse. He looked very fierce.

The aunt noticed him. He was a hard, unkind man, she decided in her mind. She had no good answer to the question about the grass in the other field.

The smaller girl was bored. She began to recite the poem 'On the Road to Mandalay'. She only knew the first line, but she put what little knowledge she had to the greatest possible use. She repeated the line over and over again in a dreamy but very loud voice. The man thought she was going to try to repeat the line aloud two thousand times without stopping.

The aunt's story

'Come over here and listen to a story,' said the aunt, after the man had given her several very annoyed looks.

The children moved without much interest towards the aunt's end of the carriage. Clearly, they did not enjoy her stories very much.

In a low, secret-sounding voice, she began a colourless and terribly boring story about a little girl who was good. The girl, she said, made friends with everyone because she was so good. She was finally saved from great danger by a number of people who admired her goodness.

'Wouldn't they have saved her if she hadn't been good?' demanded the bigger of the two girls. It was exactly the question that the man had wanted to ask.

'Well, yes,' admitted the aunt weakly, 'but I don't think they would have run quite so fast to help her if she had not been so good.'

'It's the stupidest story I've ever heard,' said the bigger of the girls. She meant it.

'I didn't listen after the first bit, it was so stupid,' said Cyril.

The smaller girl made no actual comment on the story, but she had long ago started repeating her favourite line of her favourite poem.

'You don't seem to be a success as a story-teller,' said the man suddenly.

The aunt was not pleased. She did not expect people to complain about her way of entertaining her nephew and nieces.

'It's very difficult to tell stories that children can both understand and enjoy,' she said. Her voice was cold and unfriendly.

'I don't agree with you,' said the man.

'Perhaps you would like to tell them a better story?' was the aunt's angry reply.

'Yes, you tell us a story,' demanded the bigger of the girls.

The man's story

'Once upon a time,' began the man, 'there was a little girl called Bertha, who was extraordinarily good.'

The children's interest began at once to die; all stories seemed alike, no matter who told them.

'She did all that she was told, she was always truthful, she kept her clothes clean, learned her lessons perfectly, and was polite to everyone.'

'Was she pretty?' asked the bigger of the small girls.

'Not as pretty as any of you,' said the man, 'but she was horribly good.'

The children began to change their minds about this story. The word 'horrible' in connection with goodness was something new.

'She was so good,' continued the man, 'that she won several medals for goodness, which she always wore, pinned on to the front of her dress. There was one medal for obedience, another medal for punctuality, and a third for good manners. They were large metal medals and they clinked against one another as she walked. No other child in the town where she lived had as many as three medals. So everybody knew that she must be an extra good child.'

'Horribly good,' said Cyril.

'Everybody talked about her goodness. Even the Prince of the country heard about it. He said that as she was so very good, once a week she could walk in his park, which was just outside the town. It was a beautiful park, and no children were ever allowed in it. So it was a great honour for Bertha to be allowed to go there.'

'Were there any sheep in the park?' demanded Cyril.

'No,' said the man, 'there were no sheep.'

'Why weren't there any sheep?' Cyril wanted to know.

The aunt allowed herself a smile. Now, she thought to herself, he will begin to understand how difficult it is to please these three.

Neither sheep nor clocks

'There were no sheep in the park,' said the man, 'because the Prince's mother once had a dream that her son would either be killed by a sheep or else by a clock falling on him. For that reason, the Prince never kept a sheep in his park or a clock in his palace.'

The aunt was clearly amazed.

'Was the Prince killed by a sheep or by a clock?' asked Cyril.

'He is still alive, so we can't tell whether the dream will come true,' said the man. 'Anyway, there were no sheep in the park. But there were lots of little pigs running around.'

'What colour were they?'

'Black with white faces, white with black spots, black all over, grey with white patches, and some were white all over.' The story-teller paused to let a full idea of the park and its inhabitants sink into the children's imagination; then he continued.

'Bertha was rather sorry to find that there were no flowers in the park. She had promised her aunts that she would not pick any of the kind Prince's flowers. She had meant to keep her promise, so of course it made her feel silly to find that there were no flowers to pick.'

'Why weren't there any flowers?'

'Because the pigs had eaten them all,' said the man. 'The gardeners had told the Prince that he couldn't have both pigs and flowers in the park, so he decided to have pigs and no flowers.'

The children thought the Prince had chosen correctly; so many people would have decided the other way.

LIFE'S LITTLE PROBLEMS

'There were lots of other delightful things in the park. There were ponds with gold and blue and green fish in them, and trees with beautiful parrots that said clever things, and humming birds that hummed beautiful songs. Bertha walked up and down and enjoyed herself very much. She thought to herself: "If I were not so extraordinarily good, I would never have been allowed to come into this beautiful park," and her three medals clinked against one another as she walked. They reminded her how very good she really was. Just then, a great big wolf came creeping into the park to catch a fat little pig for its supper.'

'What colour was it?' asked the children.

'Mud-colour all over, with a black tongue and pale grey eyes that shone with cruelty. The first thing that it saw in the park was Bertha; her dress was so spotlessly white and clean that it could be seen from a great distance. Bertha saw the wolf and saw that it was coming towards her. She began to wish that she had never been allowed to come into the park. She ran as hard as she could, and the wolf came after her, running faster and faster. Bertha just managed to reach some bushes and she hid herself there.

'The wolf came sniffing among the branches. Its long black tongue hung out of its mouth and its pale grey eyes glared with anger. Bertha was terribly frightened. She thought to herself: "If I had not been so extraordinarily good, I would have been in the town, now, and quite safe."

'However, the scent of the bush was so strong that the wolf could not sniff out where Bertha was hiding. And the bushes were so thick that he could not see her. So he thought he'd better go and catch a little pig instead.'

A beautiful ending

The children knew what sort of story this was. It was just like their aunt's story after all. The good little girl was safe from danger. But the man had not finished.

'Bertha, by now, was trembling very much with fear,' he continued. 'As she trembled, the medals for obedience clinked against the medals for good manners and punctuality.

'The wolf was just moving away when he heard the sound of the medals clinking. He stopped to listen. They clinked again in a bush quite near him. He jumped into the bush, his pale grey eyes shining, and dragged Bertha out and ate her up completely. All that was left were her shoes, a few bits of clothing, and the three medals for goodness.'

'Were any of the little pigs killed?' asked Cyril.

'No, they all escaped.'

'The story began badly,' said the smaller of the girls, 'but it had a beautiful ending.'

'It is the most beautiful story I've ever heard,' said the bigger of the girls, and she meant it.

'It is the only beautiful story I have ever heard,' said Cyril.

The aunt was quick to disagree.

'That was a thoroughly improper story to tell to young children. I have always taught them to be good and behave well, and your story suggests they should do the opposite!'

'At any rate,' said the man, collecting his suitcases, 'I kept them quiet for ten minutes, which was more than you were able to do.' The train came into Templecombe Station and stopped. The man got out of the carriage, closing the door behind him.

'Poor woman!' he thought to himself as he walked down the platform. 'For the next six months or so those children will want nothing but another thoroughly improper story!'

THE SPECIALISTS

ADRIAN

The Socialist

Little is known of the life of Adrian, except that he told everyone he met how hard it was. He said he worked as a salesman in a clothing store and that he lived alone in a small room in one of the poorer parts of West London. His mother lived in Bethnal Green, which was an even poorer place.

What is certain, however, is that now and then he dined with wealthy friends at the best London restaurants. On these occasions, Adrian always arrived correctly dressed, his manners and tastes were perfect, and he was usually the guest of Lucas Croyden.

Lucas had plenty of money. He had never worked a day in his life, but, like many rich and idle young men, he wanted to do something for society in his own way. He was a Socialist, which was fashionable at the time, and he set himself the task of introducing lower class men to upper class food. You could never hope to educate the masses, he argued, until you had brought plover's eggs into their lives, and taught them the difference between *coupe Jacques* and *Macédoine de fruits*.

A mad idea

It was after one of his evenings with Adrian, that Lucas walked into a tea-shop and met, quite unexpectedly, his aunt, Mrs Susan Mebberley.

'Who was that good-looking boy who was dining with you last night?' she asked. 'He looked much too nice to be thrown away on you.'

'Just a friend. You probably don't know him.' Lucas sat down at his aunt's table without waiting to be invited.

'I don't suppose I ever shall,' she said, 'unless you tell me his name.'

'Adrian,' said Lucas, trying to be as unhelpful as possible.

'And what family is he from?'

'His mother lives at Beth —'

Lucas stopped himself just in time. His aunt would not like to think he had friends whose mothers lived at Bethnal Green!

'Beth? Where is that? It sounds like a place in the Middle East. She is not with the government people, is she?'

'Oh, no. She works among the poor.'

Lucas, even at this point, managed to avoid direct untruthfulness. Adrian's mother worked in a laundry.

'I see,' said Mrs Mebberley, 'charity work of some sort. And meanwhile the young man has no one to look after him. I shall make it my special duty to see that he is properly looked after. Bring him to visit me.'

'My dear Aunt Susan,' complained Lucas, 'I really know very little about him. He may not be at all nice, you know.'

'He has delightful hair and a pleasant face. This summer I shall take him with me to Homburg.'

'Homburg? It's the maddest thing I ever heard of,' said Lucas angrily.

'Well, there is madness in our family. You may not have noticed it yourself, but I am sure all your friends have.'

And Lucas, realizing that Susan Mebberley was a woman as well as an aunt, saw that she would have to be allowed to do what she thought best.

Dohledorf

Soon afterwards, Adrian was taken abroad by Susan Mebberley and a holiday group made up of her closer friends and relations. After further thought, Homburg was avoided, and the party settled itself into the best hotel at Dohledorf, a small town in the Alps.

Dohledorf was the usual kind of small holiday town, with the usual sort of visitors, that one finds in most parts of Switzerland during the summer season, but to Adrian it was all unusual. The mountain air, the certainty of regular meals and the pleasant holiday atmosphere affected him in much the same way as the light and warmth of a green-house might affect a weed that had somehow found its way inside.

To give one small example, Adrian, who came from the poorer classes, had been brought up in a world where breaking things was regarded as a crime to be punished; it was something new and exciting to discover that if you smashed things in the right way and at the proper moment, people though you were rather amusing.

Susan Mebberley had told Lucas she was going to show Adrian a bit of the world; in the end that particular bit of the world began to see a good deal of Adrian.

Adrian's cleverness

Lucas heard about the holiday, not from his aunt or Adrian, but from the pen of Clovis, who was also with the party.

'The entertainment which Susan organized last night ended in disaster,' Clovis wrote. 'I thought it would. The youngest Grobmayer, a five-year-old, had been acting like some sort of child-angel during the early part of the evening, and was then put to bed. Adrian kidnapped it when its nurse was downstairs. Without anyone knowing what he had done, he introduced it during the second act, dressed up as a performing pig. The costume completely covered the child, and it certainly looked very like a pig. It made grunting noises just like the real thing, too. No one knew exactly who or what it was, but every one said Adrian's idea was awfully clever, especially the Grobmayers. Then, at the end, Adrian pinched the 'pig' too hard, and it yelled out 'Mama'!

'I am supposed to be good at descriptions, but don't ask me to describe what the Grobmayers said and did at that moment. It was like one of the angrier parts of an Italian opera. We are moving up the valley, to the Hotel Victoria.'

Panic

Clovis's next letter arrived five days later, and was written from the Hotel Steinbock.

'We left the Hotel Victoria this morning. It was fairly comfortable and quiet — at least there was an air of calm about it when we arrived. Before we had been there twenty-four hours, however, most of the calm had disappeared "like a beautiful dream," as Adrian expressed it.

'Nothing especially strange happened till last night, when Adrian was unable to sleep. He got up and amused himself by unscrewing all the room numbers on his floor and screwing them back on the wrong doors. He screwed the bathroom label to the door of the bedroom next to it, which was Frau Hofrath Schilling's room, and this morning, from seven o'clock onwards, the old lady had an endless stream of unexpected visitors. She was too horrified and shocked it seems to get up and lock her door. The would-be users of the bathroom rushed back in confusion to their rooms. Of course, the change of numbers led them to the wrong doors again, and the corridor gradually filled with panic-stricken humans dressed in their night-wear and running wildly about like rabbits with a fox on their tails. It took nearly an hour before the guests were all sorted back into their rooms. Frau Hofrath's condition was still causing some anxiety when we left.

'Susan is beginning to look worried. She can't throw Adrian out, as he hasn't got any money, and she can't send him to his people, as she doesn't know where they are. Adrian says his mother moves about a good deal and he has lost her address. Probably, if the truth were known, he has had an argument at home. So many young men seem to think that quarrelling with one's family is the proper thing to do.'

The next communication that Lucas received from the travellers took the form of a telegram sent 'reply pre-paid' by Mrs Mebberley herself. It consisted of a single sentence: 'In Heaven's name, where is Beth?'

THE OPEN WINDOW

A rest cure in the countryside

'My aunt will be here soon, Mr Nuttel,' said a very confident young lady of fifteen, 'but until she comes, you will just have to sit and talk with me.'

Framton Nuttel tried to say something polite. Privately, he did not want to be there at all. He was a nervous man, and had come to the countryside for a rest cure. He doubted more than ever whether these visits to total strangers would be of any help.

'I know what you will do,' his sister had said when he was preparing to leave home in London, 'you will stay in all by yourself and not speak to anyone, and when your holiday is over, you will feel worse than ever. I shall give you some letters of introduction to all the people I know there. Some of them are quite nice.'

Framton wondered whether Mrs Sappleton, the aunt to whom his sister had written one of her letters of introduction, was nice.

'Do you know many of the people round here?' asked the niece.

'Hardly anyone,' said Framton. 'My sister stayed round here, about four years ago. She wrote me a few letters of introduction to some of the people here, like your aunt.'

He made the last statement in a voice that made it clear he did not entirely agree with his sister's plan.

'Then you know almost nothing about my aunt?' continued the confident young lady.

'Only her name and address,' said the visitor. He was wondering whether Mrs Sappleton was married or a widow. Something about the room seemed to suggest that men lived there, too.

The great tragedy

'Her great tragedy happened just three years ago,' said the girl, 'that would be after your sister knew her.'

'Her tragedy?' asked Framton. In this peaceful country spot, it was hard to believe that tragedies could ever happen.

'You may wonder why we keep the French windows wide open on an October afternoon,' said the niece, as she pointed to the large double windows that opened on to a lawn.

'It is quite warm for autumn,' said Framton, 'but what have those French windows got to do with the tragedy?'

'Out through those windows, exactly three years ago today, her husband and her two young brothers went off for a day's hunting. They never came back. It had been a terribly wet summer, you know, and ground that was safe in other years had become highly dangerous. In crossing the fields, they all three fell into a marshy mud-filled hole, and were swallowed up. Their bodies were never found. That was the worst part of it.' Here the girl's voice lost its confident note and trembled with sorrow.

'Poor aunt always thinks that they will come back some day. She is sure that they and the little brown dog that was lost with them will walk in at those windows just as they used to do. That is why the French windows are kept open every evening till it is quite dark. Poor dear aunt, she has often told me how they went out, her husband with his white coat over his arm, and Ronnie, her youngest brother, singing the song, "Bertie, why do you bound?" as he always did.

Do you know, sometimes on still, quiet evenings like this, I too almost think that they will all walk in through those windows —'

She broke off with a little shudder. It was a relief to Framton when the aunt finally came into the room.

An awful topic

'I hope Vera has been amusing you?' said the aunt politely.

'She has been very interesting,' said Framton.

'I do hope you don't mind the open windows,' said Mrs Sappleton. 'My husband and brothers will be home soon, and they always come in this way. They've been out shooting birds in the marshes today, so they'll make a real mess over my poor carpets. You menfolk are so thoughtless at times, aren't you?'

She talked on cheerfully about the shooting, and hunting for ducks in the winter. To Framton it was all purely terrible. He made several unsuccessful efforts to turn the conversation to a less awful topic. He could see that his hostess was giving him only a small bit of her attention. Her eyes were constantly looking past him to the open windows and the lawn beyond. It was certainly unfortunate that he should have come to visit on this tragic date.

'The doctors have ordered me to take a complete rest, to avoid excitement, and any hard physical exercise,' said Framton, who like many other sick people thought that total strangers and new friends really want to hear all the details of one's medical problems, their causes and cures. 'On the matter of what I should eat it, though, they are not so much in agreement,' he continued.

'Is that so?' said Mrs Sappleton, in a voice which showed her boredom. Then she suddenly brightened — but not at what Framton was saying.

'Here they are at last!' she cried. 'Just in time for tea, and look at them — covered in mud right up to the eyes!'

Framton turned towards the niece with a sympathetic look. The girl was staring out through the open windows with

horror in her eyes. In a frozen shock of fear Framton turned round in his seat and looked in the same direction.

Return of the hunters

Three people were walking across the lawn towards the windows. They all carried guns, and one of them was holding a white coat over his arm. A tired, brown dog kept close at their heels. Noiselessly they came towards the house, and then a young voice sang out of the darkness: 'I said, Bertie, why do you bound?'

Framton grabbed wildly for his stick and hat; he ran so fast that he hardly remembered going through the hall-door, the garden, or the front gate. A man coming along the road on a bicycle turned, suddenly, to avoid knocking him down, and rode straight into a hedge.

'Here we are, my dear,' said the one who held the white coat, coming in through the window, 'fairly muddy, but most of it's dry. Who was that who ran out as we came in?'

'A most amazing man, a Mr Nuttel,' said Mrs Sappleton. 'He could only talk about his illnesses, and ran off without a word of goodbye or apology when you arrived. One would think he had seen a ghost.'

'I'm sure it was the dog,' said the niece calmly. 'He told me he had a horror of dogs. He said he was once chased into a graveyard somewhere in India by a pack of wild dogs, and had to spend the night in a newly-dug grave with the animals glaring at him and making awful noises just above his head. Enough to make anyone lose their nerve.'

Story-telling was her specialty.

QUESTIONS AND ACTIVITIES

CHAPTER 1

Who said these things, and who were they speaking to?

1 'It was your idea.'
2 'How clever you are. You seem to notice everything.'
3 'I won't allow it — I absolutely won't allow it.'
4 'It gets her into all sorts of trouble.'
5 'What is the name of those roses, do you know?'
6 'I don't want to have to keep it for the rest of my life.'

CHAPTER 2

Name the people these sentences are about.

1 Who ate breakfast with a black, angry look on his face?
2 Who loved shillings with a great, strong love?
3 Who locked himself in his bedroom?
4 Who knew Clovis slightly, and was rather afraid of him?
5 Who had quite a lot to explain about Venetian art?
6 Who hoped the house would catch fire?

CHAPTER 3

Correct the nine errors in this paragraph.

He was greatly worried about his own fate. He knew it was possible to live for some time in this world on three sovereigns, but to a man who was used to thinking himself unlucky if he had a few pennies to spend, it seemed a bad start. In a rather strange way, fortune had been cruel to him when he last walked down these lanes as a hopeful wanderer. As he got closer to the farm, his feelings grew higher and more hopeful. There was a sense of relief at being his old self again, and starting to act the better part of another man.

Chapter 4

Put the words at the ends of these sentences in the right order.

1. Laura had good reason for thinking she would be a
   [next] [in] [animal] [lower] [her] [life].
2. Egbert decided to get the hunting dogs
   [earliest] [the] [moment] [at] [possible].
3. Aurora felt sorry because the otter had such
   [human] [in] [eyes] [its] [a] [look].
4. The wild-looking boy said it was quite two months
   [tasted] [he] [since] [had] [child-meat].
5. Cunningham did not want to discuss anything
   [impossibly] [of] [nature] [an] [strange].
6. Van Cheele realized he could never say how
   [boy] [the] [dangerous] [was] [terribly].

Chapter 5

Put the beginnings of these sentences with the right endings.

1. If Lady Beanford caught a cold, she never
2. The servant, Robert, said that Louise
3. Matilda had never forgotten the time when the Bishop
4. When Matilda sent away the cook, the Bishop knew he
5. As soon as the tiger saw the goat, it
6. The wrong animal had been hit, and the old tiger

(a) had died of heart-failure.
(b) was no longer welcome.
(c) lay flat on the earth.
(d) let it go again.
(e) paid her an unexpected visit.
(f) had been upstairs all afternoon.

CHAPTER 6

Put these sentences in the right order. The first one is correct.

1 Groby took Miss Wepley's sweets and then threw them at her.
2 He threw his stable-boy into some stinging nettles.
3 Everyone thought Groby had saved Leonard Spabbink's life.
4 He dragged Spabbink into the bathroom.
5 He terrified the maid by banging his teeth at her.
6 He went to Spabbink's room and attacked him for snoring.
7 He overturned a candle and set the curtains on fire.

CHAPTER 7

Whose names should go in the gaps?

1 ____ knew exactly what frightened the Brogue and was prepared for anything it decided to do.
2 ____ had personally made most of the holes in the hedges for miles around.
3 ____ had a houseful of daughters and thought a husband or two would be welcome.
4 ____ said the idea that lambs are calm, gentle little creatures was entirely false.
5 ____ wanted her children not only to be taught but to be interested in what they learned.
6 ____'s friends and relations were well used to the fact of her luggage arriving without her.
7 ____ was one of those people who lose control of a situation as soon as they are seriously opposed.
8 ____ had made a mistake as to the day on which she was expected.

CHAPTER 8

Which of these statements are true, and what is wrong with the false ones?

1 Lady Ann would not speak to Egbert because she was so angry with him.

2 No one ever knew if Lady Ann felt unwell, because she never told anyone.
3 Egbert never did anything that Lady Ann could complain about.
4 Crefton told Martha Pillamon what was written up on the barn door.
5 The tea was not good to drink because the water would not boil.
6 As a visitor, Crefton did not think he would suffer from Martha Pillamon's anger.

CHAPTER 9

Which do you think are the best answers?

1 The Brimley Bomefields had nearly forgotten their aunt because (a) she was poor; (b) she lived in France; (c) she was unkind.
2 They disliked Roger because (a) he wasted his money on horse races; (b) he would get most of the aunt's money when she died; (c) he went to India.
3 They took their aunt to Dieppe in France so that she would (a) learn the truth about Roger; (b) learn to speak French; (c) learn how to gamble.
4 The aunt became (a) a good gambler and very happy; (b) a bad gambler but very happy; (c) a bad gambler and very unhappy.
5 The Brimley Bomefields blamed (a) Christine, for talking to the aunt about Roger; (b) Roger, for saying that they were all gamblers; (c) Veronique, because it was her idea to take the aunt to France.

CHAPTER 10

Put the sentences in these summaries of the stories in the right order.

He liked Rhoda because she served tea without asking endless, silly questions. James Cushat-Prinkley decided to get married. Instead he married Rhoda Ellam. His female relatives thought he would propose to Joan Sebastable. However, after they were married, Rhoda served tea in the same way as other women.

The man, too, thought the aunt was not a success as a storyteller. The children thought it was a stupid story. He told the children a story about a good little girl who was eaten by a wolf. The aunt tried to entertain her nephew and nieces by telling them a story. The children liked this story much better.

CHAPTER 11

Put the beginnings of these sentences with the right endings.

1 Now and then Adrian dined with wealthy friends at the	(a) countryside.
2 Lucas did not want to admit he had friends whose mothers lived at	(b) marshes.
3 Susan Mebberley's holiday group stayed in the best hotel at	(c) Bethnal Green.
4 Framton Nuttel was a nervous man who was taking a rest cure in the	(d) French windows.
5 The niece said she thought her dead uncles might walk in through the	(e) Dohledorf.
6 The aunt said her husband and brothers had been out shooting in the	(f) best London restaurants.

Grade 1

Alice's Adventures in Wonderland
Lewis Carroll

The Call of the Wild and Other Stories
Jack London

Emma
Jane Austen

Jane Eyre
Charlotte Brontë

Little Women
Louisa M. Alcott

The Lost Umbrella of Kim Chu
Eleanor Estes

Tales From the Arabian Nights
Edited by David Foulds

Treasure Island
Robert Louis Stevenson

The Jungle Book
Rudyard Kipling

Life Without Katy and Other Stories
O. Henry

Lord Jim
Joseph Conrad

A Midsummer Night's Dream and Other Stories from Shakespeare's Plays
Edited by David Foulds

Oliver Twist
Charles Dickens

The Talking Tree and Other Stories
David McRobbie

Through the Looking Glass
Lewis Carroll

The Stone Junk and Other Stories
D.H. Howe

Grade 2

The Adventures of Sherlock Holmes
Sir Arthur Conan Doyle

A Christmas Carol
Charles Dickens

The Dagger and Wings and Other Father Brown Stories
G.K. Chesterton

The Flying Heads and Other Strange Stories
Edited by David Foulds

The Golden Touch and Other Stories
Edited by David Foulds

Gulliver's Travels — A Voyage to Lilliput
Jonathan Swift

Grade 3

The Adventures of Tom Sawyer
Mark Twain

Around the World in Eighty Days
Jules Verne

The Canterville Ghost and Other Stories
Oscar Wilde

David Copperfield
Charles Dickens

Fog and Other Stories
Bill Lowe

Further Adventures of Sherlock Holmes
Sir Arthur Conan Doyle